Shock

Celebrity

Deaths and Murders

Volume 3

Dylan Frost

Contents

Introduction

The cases that follow are once again eclectic and darkly fascinating. Drug overdoses, murders, suicides, unsolved deaths, autoerotic asphyxiation, car crashes, plane crashes, freak accidents, doomed child stars, and so on.

Shocking Celebrity Deaths and Murders Volume 3 includes, among others, Anna Nicole Smith, Dustin Diamond, Patrick Swayze, John Ritter, Sarah Harding, Bobby Driscoll, Samantha Smith, and Mya-Lecia Naylor.

THE BLACK DAHLIA

On January 15, 1947, a body was discovered on a street in Los Angeles. The body was that of a young dark haired woman. She had been sliced in half, had her blood removed, and her mouth cut into a Joker style smile. A tattoo had been cut from her thigh and stuffed in her private parts. It was a grisly and shocking murder worthy of Jack the Ripper. The police managed - after some effort - to identify the victim through fingerprints. Her name was Elizabeth Short - though in the wake of this case she would become immortal as the Black Dahlia. The Black Dahlia mystery baffled the police. Not only was the murder brutal and gruesome it also indicated a degree of medical knowledge. The relative proximity of a medical school close to where the body was found led the police to suspect the killer might have a connection to this establishment.

The killer was deemed to be cunning, intelligent, and most likely completely insane. Elizabeth had been missing for six days when her body was found. It is presumed then that the killer kidnapped and then tortured her before the murder. The police found out that Elizabeth Short was working as a waitress at the time of her death. Like so many people she had moved to Los Angeles to become a star but she found that acting jobs were hard to come by and so she ended up waiting tables to make ends meet. That was a familiar story for those who go to Hollywood dreaming of fame.

About a week after the grisly discovery of the body, a letter was sent to the local newspaper containing some of Elizabeth Short's personal belongings. The contents had been cleaned with petrol - which was also how the killer had cleaned Short's body before he dissected it. It was pretty obvious then that the sender of this letter was the killer. How else would they have Elizabeth Short's personal affects? The police, thanks partly to these personal affects, manage to obtain the details of dozens of men that Elizabeth Short had known but investigations into these men turned out to be a frustrating dead end. The case eventually went cold. The killer was never caught. There are theories though. One theory contends that Short's murder was connected to The Cleveland Torso Murderer.

The Cleveland Torso Murderer is one of the grisliest serial killers never captured. Some suspect that this killer might have murdered Elizabeth Short. The killer was active from 1935 to 1938 and killed between twelve and twenty victims. This killer killed both men and women - which is rare for serial killers because they usually target the gender they are attracted to (which is overwhelmingly females because the vast majority of serial killers turn out to be straight men). The targets were chosen very carefully in that they were drifters or homeless people so wouldn't be missed. The victims were dismembered and beheaded. The male victims were castrated. Some of the victims had a chemical agent applied to them.

The Cleveland Torso Murderer is credited with twelve official murders but may have killed twenty people in all. There is a theory that this may have been the work of more than one killer but the truth was never really established. The famous lawman Eliot Ness was in charge of the investigation to catch the killer. At one point the killer even left the remains of one victim outside of the office building where Ness worked - simply to taunt Ness. Because the bodies were often found some time after death and many of the heads had been removed this made identification of the victims almost impossible at times. In fact, only a couple of victims were ever identified.

The main suspect in the case was Dr Francis Sweeney. It is said that Ness thought Sweeney was the killer. Sweeney was a former medic in the army who had performed amputations in combat zones. Sweeney also failed a lie detector test when he was in police custody. However, Sweeney was never charged or prosecuted for the murders - apparently because Ness thought there was little chance of securing a conviction. One thing that complicated matters was that Dr Sweeney was a cousin of Congressman Martin L. Sweeney. Congressman Martin L. Sweeney was known for his dislike of Eliot Ness and wouldn't have taken too kindly to these murders being pinned on a relative.

Dr Sweeney was therefore not put on trial. He was bitter at his treatment by Ness and sent Ness threatening letters until he died. A man named Frank Dolezal was actually arrested for the murders and had a confession beaten out of him but it transpired that he was innocent. Dolezal is believed to attracted suspicion because he knew one of the victims. The question of who The Cleveland Torso Murderer really was therefore remains a mystery. All we really do know is that this was an especially disturbed and grisly killer who clearly enjoyed the attention his crimes were affording him. He was one of the deadliest serial killers never to be captured.

The same year that Elizabeth Short was murdered, a woman named Jeanne French was found dead in Los Angeles. She had been stomped to death and a cryptic message was scrawled on her body in lipstick. Some believe that the deaths of Short and French are connected and that they both encountered the same killer. The police did not believe in this theory themselves though and felt these two deaths were not connected but simply disconnected tragedies. Naturally, the police had to deal with a lot of time wasters during their investigation into Short's murder. Many people came forward to claim they had killed Elizabeth Short but were then revealed to be fantasists or liars. There are a number of genuine suspects in the Elizabeth Short murder case but the actual killer has never been verified.

Among the Black Dahlia suspects are Walter Bayley. Bayley was a surgeon who lived only a few minutes away from where Short's body was found. He was suffering from a degenerative brain disease at the time. This has led to a theory that he was acting in a crazy unhinged manner and might have been capable of murder. The counter argument is that the 67 year-old Bayley was not really in any fit state to carry out a murder like this - which would have required planning, stealth, and physical strength. Bayley's status as a Black Dahlia suspect comes from the fact that he had medical training (so would have known how to dissect a body) and also easy access to properties in the area where Short was disposed of.

Another suspect was a bellhop and former mortician's assistant named Leslie Dillon. Dillon began writing to Los Angeles Police Department psychiatrist Dr. J. Paul De River with his theories about Short's murder. Dillon's detailed knowledge of the case and obvious dark fascination with sex and sadism led the police to believe he could well be a suspect. Dillon even claimed he knew the man that had killed Elizabeth Short. Dr. J. Paul De River took this claim to be a proxy confession by Dillon. Dillon was placed in custody at one point and many detectives came to suspect he was the killer. The stumbling block though was that Dillon's whereabouts at the time of the murder could not be proven. It could not be established that he was in Los Angeles and so there was no case against him without this vital evidence. You can only convict someone of a murder if you have some proof that they were actually in the place where the murder took place!

Another suspect in Short's death was Mark Hansen. Hansen was a nightclub owner and Elizabeth Short's landlord. It transpired that he was one of the last people she spoke to before she went missing. The police believed that Hansen was infatuated with Short but she'd rebuffed his romantic and sexual advances. What made the police especially interested in Hansen was that he was friends with a number of doctors and there was evidence that as a young man he had attended a medical school. One can see how these details, when factored in with his personal connection to Elizabeth Short, made Hansen a person of interest. Mark Hansen died in 1964. He was never charged with Short's murder. The police detectives from the time and in recent years who have studied the case seem to have conflicting views concerning Hansen as a suspect. Some believe he murdered Short and others think he was a red herring who had nothing to do with the case.

Patrick O'Reilly was an interesting suspect in the Black Dahlia murder case. O'Reilly was a doctor who was friends with Mark Hansen. They apparently visited sex parties together. It seems reasonable to presume then that O'Reilly must have known Elizabeth Short. O'Reilly had criminal charges for violent sexually motivated crimes and he certainly had the medical knowledge required to dissect and clean a dead body. Despite all of these apparent connective details though he was never charged with having anything to do with Short's murder. O'Reilly was married to the daughter of a police captain. This has led to theories of a police cover-up.

George Hodel was also a suspect and placed under police surveillance at one point in relation to the murder of Elizabeth Short. Hodel was a physician accused of raping his teenage daughter. He was known to be a dodgy and troubled sort of character. The police manage to get some evidence that Elizabeth Short may have been one of George Hodel's patients. In the end though the evidence collected was not sufficient for a formal charge or a trial. Steve Hodel, George HJodel's son, later wrote a book in which he claimed his father was the killer of Elizabeth Short. Steve Hodel then rather damaged what little credibility he had by writing another book in which he claimed his father was also the Zodiac killer. These books were taken with what you might describe as a pinch of salt. I daresay Hodel is now working on a book claiming his father had access to a time machine and was Jack the Ripper.

George Knowlton is often listed as a Black Dahlia murder suspect - thanks mainly to the efforts of his daughter. Janice Knowlton claimed that her father George murdered and dissected Elizabeth Short in their garage. Janice Knowlton (inevitably) wrote a book about this and said that Elizabeth Short was a sex worker who would find children for child abuse gangs. Janice Knowlton claimed that she was later sold to a sex gang herself and ended up being abused by no lesser figure than Walt Disney. Janice Knowlton died in a prescription drugs overdose in 2004. The police - you will not be surprised to hear - were never terribly convinced by her outlandish claims concerning her father although they did arrange a dig at her childhood home. Nothing suspicious relating to a murder was found on the property though.

Other theories include the possibility that Elizabeth Short was killed by a woman that she may have been sharing a room with and fallen out with. This theory doesn't explain though why this disgruntled room mate would have then undertook such a grisly and complicated - not to mention risky - manner of disposing of the body. Donald H. Wolfe wrote in his 2006 book The Mob, the Mogul, and the Murder That Transfixed Los Angeles, that Elizabeth Short was murdered by the gangster Bugsy Siegel at the request of newspaper publisher Norman Chandler. Short, so the theory goes, was pregnant with Chandler's child and so Chandler wanted to get rid of her.

There is no evidence though which connects Bugsy Siegel to the murder of Elizabeth Short. The craziest theory concerning this murder was that proposed by a childhood friend of Elizabeth Short.

He concluded that the killer in this awful case was none other than the film director Orson Welles! The real truth about the Black Dahlia case has yet to be verified. It's a case which seems set to keep armchair detectives busy for many years to come.

HECTOR CAMACHO

Héctor (Macho) Camacho was born in Bayamón, Puerto Rico in 1962. When he was about three his family moved to New York and he grew up in Spanish (East) Harlem. Camacho was a tearaway as a youngster constantly getting into trouble and had a spell in prison when he was fifteen. Life on the streets as a petty criminal seemed to be his destiny. That all changed though when he was encouraged to try boxing by a high school teacher. Camacho was a natural when it came to the sweet science. He had cat like reflexes and fists that moved faster than a laser beam. He had great movement too and could dazzle his opponents with footwork and constant motion. Camacho had a great ring IQ too - which is something you can't really teach a boxer. Hector Camacho was at home in the ring and knew exactly what he was doing inside that squared circle.

Camacho won three Golden Gloves and only lost four times in 100 amateur fights. It was professional boxing though that Camacho craved because it was in the pro ranks where the money is made. His ambition was to buy his mother a house. He turned professional in 1980 and claimed he could already beat the great featherweight champions Salvador Sánchez and Eusebio Pedroza. In reality though he would have to wait five years for a title shot. Camacho was taken under the wing of networks like CBS and HBO - who believed he was destined for superstardom. He was certainly a huge attraction in the early to mid eighties.

Camacho was something of a pioneer when it came to the showbusiness elements of boxing. It was Camacho who first did those crazy theatrical ring entrances which the likes of Prince Naseem Hamed would later mimic. Camacho would wear sequinned glittery trunks (or even a toga) and come to the ring dressed as a Roman centurion and he was simultaneously an interviewer's dream and nightmare. A dream in that he was funny, brash, and charismatic. A nightmare in that he was not the most politically correct of people and so was liable to say something crass or offensive from time to time. It was all box-office gold though and built Camacho into a big star. "Over the years, people have said I'm crazy," Camacho said. "And I am. Crazy like a fox. My act is a smart one. It sold lots of tickets."

By the time he won the WBC super-featherweight title in 1985, Camacho was considered to be one of the best pound for pound fighters in the world. Camacho then moved up in weight and won a portion of the world lightweight championship in 1985 but his boxing career was never quite the same after his 1986 fight with the hard-hitting Edwin Rosario. Camacho had been used to having things his own way in the ring but Rosario hurt him badly several times and Camacho barely escaped with a disputed split-decision. Camacho's nickname 'Macho' seemed highly inappropriate from here on in because Camacho's style now became safety first. He seemed far more interested in not being hit than entertaining the crowd. While that was sensible enough from a strategic (and health) point of view it unavoidably meant that his star began to wane.

Camacho's boxing career became more sporadic and rather than chase champions and titles he was more interested in sideshow 'event' fights - like his bout with a comebacking Ray Mancini or his clash with the oft beaten but marketable Italian-American slugger Vinnie Pazienza. When Camacho fought Pazienza in 1990 the pre-fight hoopla reached almost epic proportions of bad taste. Camacho brought a Pazienza Voodo doll to one press conference which he daubed in tomato sauce (like many white boxers Pazienza was a notorious bleeder) while Pazienza, amongst other things, threw a sanitary napkin at Camacho and managed to insult 'gay activists' when he made some politically incorrect references to his opponent's dress sense. When he was obliged to apologise to the groups he'd offended he made his apology in a deliberately effeminate voice and insulted them all over again.

Camacho's main problem was drugs. He was hooked on cocaine and it was sometimes almost impossible to get him into training camp. Despite his fame, Camacho never quite managed to leave the street life of his youth behind. "Macho always believed that his career was going to continue (even after his drug dependency became more prevalent)," said a confident. "He got caught in that tide, in that riff, that his only companion was cocaine. Let me replace the fight with cocaine, let me hang out with cocaine. Cocaine is there for me. It's not going to disappoint me. I don't have to call cocaine 20,000 times and listen to a lie that the contract's on its way, I've got a fight (the promoter) is working on. It's the only thing that was consistent. It never let him down."

Although he never fufilled the promise he showed as a young fighter, Camacho had a long career and engaged in huge fights with the likes of Julio Cesar Chavez, Oscar De La Hoya, and Felix Trinidad (Camacho lost all of these fights on points). Héctor was a promoter's dream because he would always make the press conferences and the build-up to a fight eventful and a bit crazy - thus helping to sell more tickets. Although he fought into his forties, Camacho was always still crafty enough not to take too much punishment. He ended with a record of 79 wins and 6 losses. The losses all came when he was past his best. Camacho fought until 2010 - although trouble continued to dog him. In 2005 he was arrested for trying to rob a store. He was found to have the drug ecstasy on him at the time.

Camacho went back to Puerto Rico after he retired and was involved in some reality television shows. He had several children and his son Héctor Jr was a decent boxer too. Father and son sometimes fought on the same shows. They even joked about fighting each other and both were probably crazy enough to have done so had they been offered enough money! Camacho, despite his brash image, seemed genuinely touched whenever he was given an award or boxing honour. He meant a lot to the people of Puerto Rico. He was known as the Puerto Rican Ali to them. Sadly though, there wasn't a happy ending for Héctor Camacho. He never got make old bones and enjoy his status as a legend for very long.

Héctor Camacho's life came to a strange and sudden end on November 20, 2012 when he was shot while in his car on Puerto Rico Highway 167, in Bayamón. Camacho was in the passenger seat when a passing van was used by the gunman to fire the fatal shots.

One of the bullets hit Camacho in the mandible and the bullet then lodged in his shoulder and starved oxygen to his brain. He went into cardiac arrest and was put in a coma. At first it was reported that he would live but be paralysed. Even this prognosis though turned out to be optimistic.

Héctor's mother had to make the painful but humane decision to take him off life support. He was brain dead and had no chance of recovery. Camacho was 50 years old when he died.
Camacho was only worth about $100,000 at the time of his death - which was remarkable when you think of how long he boxed and how many millions he generated. He simply hadn't looked after his money. It was largely wasted on drugs, lavish spending, and hangers on. Incredibly, Camacho had not officially retired from boxing when he died. He may well have fought again had he lived!

Also in the car was Camacho's friend Adrian Mojica Moreno. Moreno was a drug dealer and pimp by all accounts. He also died from gunshots. In fact, he was most likely the target that day. Camacho was evidently in the car to score drugs. As for who killed Héctor, well that was a mystery until five years later when five men were named by the police - two of whom had since died. Hector's mother decided that her son should be laid to rest in New York where he had grown up. There was a big turnout of legendary boxers at his funeral. Felix Trinidad, Wilfred Benítez, and Wilfredo Gómez were among the mourners. Héctor was laid to rest Saint Raymond's New Cemetery and Mausoleum in the Bronx.

CHYNA

Joan Marie Laurer was born in 1969. She earned a languages degree and her battery of early jobs included a stint as a belly dancer. Laurer was 5'10 and obsessed with fitness and the gym. She entered fitness competitions and her statuesque appearance drew the attention of World Wrestling Federation (WWF - now known as the WWE) performers Paul "Triple H" Levesque and Shawn Michaels after a professional wrestling show in 1996. Laurer was drafted into the WWF and became the first female superstar of wrestling as 'Chyna' -

her character billed as the Ninth Wonder of the World.

With her strength and size, Chyna was the standout of the women wrestlers (Laurer once said she didn't like wrestling other women because she was frightened she might hurt them) and managed to attain a number of juicy 'storylines' in the WWF to make her one of the most famous faces on television. She made acting appearances in TV shows like 3rd Rock from the Sun, Relic Hunter, and Sabrina the Teenage Witch. She posed for Playboy and appeared on big chatshows. At the height of her WWF fame, Laurer was making over $1 million a year.

It all started to go wrong for Laurer around the time that her relationship with Paul "Triple H" Levesque ended. In 2001 she was offered $400,000 a year to sign a new WWF contract but - in a crazy decision - decided that this wasn't enough money and turned it down. "Joanie told me a few years later that she regretted it," said Laurer's sister. "The WWE was the only place where she was ever accepted. Once she lost that, she fell into a hole. And she never could climb out of it." Laurer was onto a good thing with the wrestling and should have embraced the financial security it provided. She obviously wasn't thinking straight to turn her back on it.

Laurer was banned from using the name Chyna when she left the WWF because that name/character was a trademark of the company. Laurer had a simple and effective method for getting around this. She simply changed her name to Chyna! She didn't want to go by the name Joan Marie Laurer because no one knew who that was. Chyna was sort of like a character that Laurer created - though where Chyna stopped and Joan Marie began was impossible to say in the end. Strange trivia - Laurer's first breast implants were ruptured in the ring during a wrestling match. Feel free to wheel that fact out at dinner parties if you are ever stuck for conversation.

Laurer said she had a bad relationship with her parents and never really saw them. She didn't get on with her siblings either so she always felt quite alone in the world.

Without the stability of her WWF family and regular work, Laurer to began to fall into a spiral of drug and alcohol abuse. She would go on dangerous drinking benders and lose days at a time to crystal meth. The drugs began to have a detrimental affect on both her mind and her body.

Laurer's hopes of a real acting career hadn't come to much. Appearances in straight to video films like Illegal Aliens with her friend (the equally doomed) Anna Nicole Smith were hardly likely to send her to the Hollywood A-list. Laurer was reportedly considered for the part of the 'Terminatrix' in Terminator 3: Rise of the Machines but lost out on the role to Kristanna Loken (who was a much more experienced actress). It was Arnold Schwarzenegger who threw Laurer's hat into the ring because he was a big wrestling fan.

In 2004, Laurer featured in a porn film called 1 Night in China - which was a sextape Laurer and her ex-boyfriend, the wrestler Sean Waltman, had sold to Red Light District Video. The film featured the duo taking a tour of China and having drug addled sex in hotel rooms. It sold 100,000 copies. There was a sequel too - titled Another Night in China. I would have suggested High Road to China as the title of the third film but this grim franchise came to an end because Laurer and Waltman had evidently run out of material. They must have been like Blake Edwards on one of those later Pink Panther films, desperately trying to cobble together old unused footage into a new film.

Laurer said she'd never had any plans or aspirations to feature in porn but she was 'making lemonade out of lemons'. If a sex tape of her was floating around then she might as well make some money out of it. That was her attitude. The subtext of this depressing tangent in her life was plainly that Laurer was struggling to find ways to make money away from wrestling. Playboy was no longer interested in Laurer, a music career bombed, and acting work was now impossible to find.

Laurer, once so famous, was now consigned to the celebrity D-list. The only place D-list celebrities find work is reality television. So Laurer appeared on shows like Celebrity Rehab. By 2011, Laurer was so strapped for cash and work she signed a contract with Vivid Video to make porn films, appearing in several movies (she inevitably played She-Hulk in the Avengers porn parody - talk about typecasting). It was a rather sad and depressing career move for someone who had once been wealthy and the idol of millions of children on mainstream television. Laurer's once fantastically successful life and career had descended into a sad parody of a star who falls right back down to the bottom again thanks to bad decisions, drugs, and booze.

Laurer's public and social media appearances started to become ever more incoherent and rambling. There was a bizarre incident where she moved to Japan and inflicted knife wounds on herself and she continued to abuse drugs and alcohol as her family became ever more distant. In 2016, Laurer died of an overdose of alcohol, combined with the anxiety drugs diazepam and nordazepam, painkillers oxycodone and oxymorphone, and the sleeping aid temazepam. She was 46 years-old. Her body was found in her apartment in Redondo Beach, California, by her manager Anthony Anzaldo. He had become concerned because Laurer hadn't talked to him or done any social media updates for several days. He knew something must be wrong.

There was a big memorial service for Laurer in Los Angeles. There were people from the world of wrestling, fans, actors, famous friends. Tributes were paid and there was a concert too. They all came together to celebrate someone who had been a great inspiration to female wrestlers in particular. On this bittersweet night Joan Marie Laurer - better known as the ring superstar Chyna - was the centre of attention once again. She was finally back in the mainstream. Laurer's ashes were scattered in the Pacific Ocean after her death. In 2019 she was a posthumous and well-deserved inductee into the WWE Hall of Fame.

PETER COOK

Peter Cook was born in Devon in 1937. Cook was a man who seemed to accomplish so much at an early age that he could never think of anything to do for an encore or even be bothered. Cook went from hip young thing with the world at his feet to a shambling alcoholic living an amusingly bohemian but melancholic existence in Hampstead phoning up late night local radio shows and pretending to be a Norwegian fisherman. Cook's father was a distinguished diplomat and the young Peter Cook was groomed for a career in the British Foreign Office. He grew up into a gangling, almost dandified figure and was affected by childhood loneliness.

At Cambridge it quickly dawns on everyone that Peter Cook is a unique character. He spends one evening extemporising on the subject of gravel until everyone is in tears of laughter. Peter hated pomposity and artificiality and drifted into comedy and performing. The plans for a career in the Foreign Office are abandoned by Cook - although it leaves him with a lingering sense of guilt. "I remember people like Leon Brittan," Cook said. "22 years-old, running around like a 44 year-old making the same points they're still making. It's a bit distressing to find them running the country. They were all so self-important in their twenties you'd have thought they'd have grown out of it."

Life at Cambridge in the late fifties was interesting for Cook, especially as he began to meet contemporaries who would go on to be famous like himself. When John Bird meets Cook he goes around telling everyone he's just met the funniest man in Britain. One man slightly skewered in the Cook story is David Frost. At Cambridge Frost is an ambitious but mediocre comedian/performer who everyone apparently thinks is a bit of an idiot. He worships Cook and eventually steals most of his act - with Cook's satirical style inspiring the television show That Was The Week That Was. "They loathed David Frost those Footlights people," said a friend of Cook. "He was a figure of fun to a whole generation. They loathed everything about him."

Cook is soon writing plays and the toast of the town. He meets three unknown young men called Dudley Moore, Jonathan Miller and Alan Bennett in a Euston restaurant in 1960 to propose they work together on a comedy stage show - the meeting leading of course to Beyond the Fringe. Beyond the Fringe becomes a huge cult hit and breaks down barriers. A famous incident, remembered as electrifying at the time for those who were there, came when Cook impersonated Harold Macmillan while Macmillan was in the audience - "When

Peter arrived on stage as Macmillan the Prime Minister's smile contorted into a rictus grin."

The impact of Beyond the Fringe was huge and the relationships between the four are interesting. It seems that Cook and Moore were much closer as natural comedians, whereas Miller and Bennett were somewhat on the outside as comedy was never their first love but more of a distraction from loftier ambitions. There was also Peter Cook's short lived Establishment Club of the early sixties, a hip hangout where Dudley Moore would play the piano,

Somerset Maugham was a member and comedians like Lenny Bruce would perform. Ned Sherrin had wanted Cook or someone from the Establishment Club to host That Was The Week That Was. Cook declined but suggested the title. Later, Cook was deeply annoyed to see that David Frost is chosen as the host of That Was The Week That Was and even using some old sketches they worked on at Cambridge.

During the Beyond the Fringe season in New York, Cook met a host of stars including JFK and Elizabeth Taylor. Cook and his first wife Wendy go to see a young comedian called Woody Allen perform and meet Noel Coward at a party. Cook was a very dashing figure in his youth. Cook became equally well known for Not Only But Also, the sketch series he performed with Dudley Moore. Dudley's Moore's penchant for cracking up during sketches became irresistible to Cook so he'd make Dudley 'corpse' on purpose.

When Cook and Moore toured Australia, Cook's drunkeness began to fray their relationship. Cook drove Moore mad on one occasion by turning up drunk for their show but then being word perfect onstage! Sadly, a number of episodes of Not Only But Also were lost because in those days the BBC used to tape over shows once they'd been transmitted. The idea that someone might want to watch these shows in the future was a concept that no one had seemed to grasp back then. As a consequence of this Peter Cook is a more cultish sort of comedian than many who followed because some of his work is more obscure - or completely lost in some cases.

Cook and Moore made a pretty good film with 1967's Bedazzled, a comic retelling of the Faust legend. The duo were also in the movie Monte Carlo or Bust! Peter's hopes for film stardom though were dented when he took the lead role in the 1970 comedy film The Rise and Rise of Michael Rimmer. Cook's performance in the film was panned and his hopes of becoming a leading man vanished. Later in 1978, Pete and Dud were in a comedy version of The Hound of the Baskervilles directed by Paul Morrissey of Andy Warhol fame. The film got atrocious reviews and wasn't even released in the United States.

Cook also founded the satirical magazine Private Eye. He was a great boss by all accounts because he would leave them alone and just pop into the office now and again - doubtless a bit worse for wear - and make them laugh. Cook's decline began in the seventies and he lost all ambition around the age of 33. He ends up doing the infamous 'Derek and Clive' tapes with Dudley Moore. Moore follows Cook around like a Chihuahua but there is an incredible twist when Dudley, to the suprise of everyone, leaves Cook behind and becomes a Hollywood star after being cast in the film '10' by Blake Edwards.

A few years later, Dudley was nominated for an Oscar for the film Arthur. Imagine how Peter Cook felt when he heard that news. His sidekick was now an Oscar nominated Hollywood movie star! Dudley also earned a Golden Globe nomination for the film Six Weeks. Dudley was a pretty big star for most of the 1980s and starred in films like Santa Claus: The Movie, Micki & Maude, and Lovesick. Cook, who was presumed in the early days to be the tall, handsome, funny one destined for movie stardom, is gobsmacked by Moore's sudden Hollywood fame. Just to rub salt into the wound, Dudley even became a sex symbol!

It was always Cook's dream to be a movie star but, as brilliant as he was at improvisation and sketches, he was a hopelessly wooden actor with no range. "Was Peter Cook unhappy, was Peter Cook jealous?" said John Lloyd. "Well, inevitably - you know, your best friend becomes one of the biggest stars in the Hollywood universe." Others have said that Cook wasn't bothered by Dudley's success and didn't care. You can't help thinking though that Cook must have looked at Dudley and felt that should have been him.

Cook, allegedly jealous at Moore's American success, ends up in a short lived American sitcom called The Two of Us playing a sarcastic English butler just so he can say that he worked in America like Dudley. Cook also had small roles in Yellowbeard and Supergirl in the early 1980s but these two films both bombed. Cook mostly did television and stage performances after this (reuniting with Dudley for comedy benefit concerts) but did appear in the cult 1987 film The Princess Bride.

Cook's final years in the eighties and nineties saw him as a somewhat bloated and sozzled figure popping up on chat shows here and there. Cook attempted to stave off boredom by drinking, making prank calls, devouring late night television, shuffling into town in a pair of slippers, marrying again and, in his last hurrah, a very funny appearance on the Clive Anderson show as four different characters. His funniest performances and riffs were now almost purely for the benefit of his eccentric friend Rainbow George at some unearthly hour in Cook's living room.

Cook got sober again when he married his last wife Chiew Lin Chong but apparently his mother's death hit him hard and made him start drinking again. Cook was the sort of person who would drink beer for breakfast and he was a notorious vodka fiend. All of the drinking eventually took a toll on his looks and health. In January, 1995, Peter Cook suffered a gastrointestinal bleeding and began coughing up blood. His liver was failing after all those years of drinking.

Cook went into a coma and died at the Royal Free Hospital in Hampstead. He was 57 years-old. It was a great loss for comedy because the Clive Anderson Show special showed that Cook could still summon up his old brilliance. Many believe that if he could have stopped drinking he could have continued to make us laugh for many more years. Peter Cook, as Stephen Fry said, decided though to leave the party early.

When he heard that Peter Cook had died, Dudley Moore said the first thing he did was ring Cook's house just so he could hear Peter's voice on the answerphone one last time. Cook was cremated at Golders Green Crematorium and his ashes were buried in an unmarked plot behind St John-at-Hampstead. There were many famous faces at Peter's memorial service and Dudley Moore performed "Goodbyee' - a comic song they used to sing at the piano at the end of their sketch show. In 1999, the minor planet 20468 Petercook, in the main asteroid belt, was named after Cook. "There was never a satire movement," said Jonathan Miller of Peter Cook. "Only the Cook empire."

JOAN CRAWFORD

Joan Crawford was born in San Antonio, Texas. Her year of birth though remained a mystery. It is presumed that crafty old Joan knocked a few years off her real age. Joan Crawford's real name was Lucille LeSueur. She hated the name Joan Crawford but it was imposed on her by the studio. There was actually a competition to come up with this name. The Hollywood bigwigs didn't like the name LeSueur because it sounded like 'sewer'. Crawford began her career as a dancer but then moved into film. Her first break came when she was a body double in the 1925 film Lady of the Night. According to legend, Joan Crawford had her back teeth removed to give her cheekbones a more prominent look. She was told by an agent that if she didn't do this she would never get any work beyond the age of 25. By the end of the 1920s, Joan Crawford was the premiere 'flapper' IT girl of the age.

Joan Crawford, according to gossip and her own suggestive comments, was famous for sleeping around as a young sex symbol. Bette Davis once famously joked that Joan Crawford had slept with every star on the MGM lot except Lassie. There is a rumour about Crawford, often reported as fact, that she made some 'stag' porn films to pay the bills before she became famous and that these films were then tracked down and destroyed to protect her later on. Legend has it that some copies still exist in private collections. The titles of said films were The Casting Couch, Velvet Lips, and The Plumber.

The popular myth is that Hollywood fixer Eddie Mannix spent exhaustive years tracking down all prints of the films and paid

$100,000 out of studio coffers for the original negative. Despite the many accounts of this alleged affair, it's highly possible that the Crawford sex film story was merely a phantom one. Perhaps they never existed - at least not in the explicit form that is often reported. It's just about possible they were tamer affairs that Crawford barely featured in. The Crawford sex film story though feels a lot like a Hollywood urban myth that caught hold and never quite got debunked. Vague whispers that the FBI knew of the films only adds to the legend, true or otherwise.

Joan Crawford was married four times and adopted five children (one of whom was reclaimed by their biological parent). Her first marriage was to the actor Douglas Fairbanks Jr. They were both very young and the marriage didn't last long. Douglas Fairbanks Jr was interested in high society and hobnobbing famous friends but Joan was more focused on her career and found all that other stuff boring. It is said she an affair with Clark Gable while they were married. Joan Crawford, like most Hollywood stars, was paranoid about gaining weight. It was reported that as part of her diet her lunch consisted of few tablespoonfuls of cold consomme, a dish of rhubarb and half a dozen crackers.

Believe it or not, it was fairly common for studios in Old Hollywood to arrange for abortions if any of their contracted actresses got pregnant - especially if the pregnancy happened out of wedlock or through an affair. Bette Davis, Joan Crawford, Judy Garland, Tallulah Bankhead, Jeanette McDonald, Lana Turner, and Dorothy Dandridge all had abortions arranged by the studios. The reason for the abortions was that the studios at the time inserted a 'morality clause' into the contracts of their stars. If an actress was involved in a scandalous (by the standards of the era) pregnancy, then this meant they had violated that morality clause.

By now, Hollywood had made the transition from silent films to 'talkies'. Joan Crawford navigated this change with flying colours because she had extensive elocution lessons. Crawford was a huge star well into the 1930s but at some point her career peaked and she was never quite as big again. As a young Hollywood star though Crawford had a level of success and fame that most actors can only dream of. Her star burned brighter than most.

Joan began adopting children in the end and this later came under some scrutiny because the adoptions were from the Tennessee Children's Home Society operated by Georgia Tann.

Georgia Tann was born in 1891 in Philadelphia, Mississippi. As a young woman she was social worker and then worked at the Mississippi Children's Home Society. Tann was apparently fired from this establishment and along with her (secret) lover Ann Atwood landed on her feet when she became Executive Secretary at the Tennessee Children's Home Society.

In those days it was a lot easier to adopt children than it is today. Adoption was fairly inexpensive and background checks were minimal. This naturally seems rather chilling to us today and, unfortunately, it sometimes was. Tann, along with various accomplices who included corrupt judges and criminal nurses, would basically abduct children to put up for adoption. Many of these children suffered dreadful abuse (not least from Tann herself - who was a child molester). To the outside world though Tann was a nice old lady who was considered to be an expert on child care. First Lady Eleanor Roosevelt even praised Tann. The actual truth was rather different.

Georgia Tann was involved in trafficking thousands of babies - many of them were stolen. Some of these babies ended up with celebrity clients like Joan Crawford. While the babies and children were awaiting adoption they were left at the Tennessee Children's Home Society. Many of the children there were neglected, sexually molested, or allowed to die. We don't really know how many deaths Georgia Tann's business was responsible for but some have suggested it might be in the hundreds.

'Many were drugged and starved by Tann and her employees,' wrote Criminal Element. 'Medical treatment was withheld. Several, perhaps hundreds, died from neglect and were buried in unmarked graves without death certificates. It has been reported that Memphis had the highest child mortality rate in the country at one time, much of which was attributed to Tann's neglect. Even those who were desirable weren't safe. Many reported later that they had been repeatedly assaulted by Tann and her employees, often strung up by the wrists while punished or sexually molested.'

Although some of the babies and children were found decent homes there were also cases of girls being adopted by paedophiles or boys being adopted to be used as slave labour on farms. How did this awful state of affairs manage to exist? The simple fact is that Georgia Tann was friends with the local judge and the Mayor. She had influence. As a consequence of this, no one scrutinised her affairs too closely. There was little paperwork in the adoptions so the real source of these children was masked. Tann is believed to have made over one million dollars from stealing and selling babies.

In 1950, Tennessee governor Gordon Browning launched an investigation into Georgia Tann after hearing stories about her adoption business. However, Tann died of cancer at the age of 59 only days before charges were due to be brought against her. Because of this there was no trial or prosecution and much of Tann's life is still shrouded in a degree of mystery. There were no prosecutions and - sadly - none of the black market children were returned to their real mothers. The dead children and babies found in the Children's Home in unmarked graves could not be identified.

In 2015, a memorial to Tann's hundreds of victims was placed in Memphis's Elmwood Cemetery. Georgia Tann was a truly awful woman and she had been hiding in plain sight all along. It was later established, thankfully, that the two children Joan Crawford had adopted from Tann were fostered legally. These two children later found their biological relatives and it was confirmed that they hadn't been stolen at birth or anything like that. It was obviously quite embarrassing for Joan Crawford in the end though to be associated with a dodgy character like Georgia Tann.

As she got a bit older and her began to fade in Hollywood, Joan Crawford started doing television and radio. Television was new at the time and American television seemed to be obsessed with anthology shows. This provided a lot of work for actors who were over the hill or out of favour with the film studios. Joan's last husband Alfred Steel was the chairman of Pepsi-Cola. Joan did a lot of promotion for Pepsi as a consequence. Steel died in 1959 from heart trouble and Joan inherited his money. Bette Davis, naturally, always made sure to pointedly drink Cocoa-Cola when she was around Joan.

Joan is still famous for her legendary feud with Davis. It was the stuff of legend. 'These forever-linked Hollywood icons took different roads to stardom,' wrote History.Com. 'Joan (born Lucille LeSueur) escaped an impoverished, hardscrabble childhood by becoming a dancer, eventually making her way to MGM studio, where she specialized in roles that played up her new persona as the scrappy, yet glamorous star. Ruth Davis (nicknamed Betty as a kid), attended boarding school and worked on Broadway but initially struggled to break through in La La Land, due in part to her perceived lack of sex appeal and steadfast refusal to play by the rules of the Hollywood system (thought she would go on to win two Oscars and garner 10 nominations in all). Bette was considered by most the better actress, while Joan was undoubtedly the bigger star, but the two found themselves pitted against each other throughout their careers.

'They also reportedly fought over the same men, with Crawford's marriage to Davis' former flame cited by many as the origin story of the bad blood. Things got even trickier when the two wound up working at the same studio, putting them in direct competition for roles. Davis and Crawford did little to dispel rumours of their ill feelings, offering up scathing comments on each other to an eager press, including classics such as Crawford's oh-so-kind attack on her rival's acting, "She's a phony, but I guess the public likes that." And so it went for decades. And so it would likely have remained if Hollywood's notorious penchant for ageism hadn't gotten in the way. By the early 1960s both of their careers were on a steep decline as roles simply dried up. So when Joan offered Bette a part in a film adaptation of the novel "What Ever Happened to Baby Jane," the once unthinkable happened, and the two agreed to co-star as sisters locked in their own macabre battle for control.

'But rather than calming the waters between the two, production on the film kicked the feud into an insane overdrive. Tales of one-upmanship ran wild and there were accusations of physical and heavy psychological abuse on both sides. The film was a hit, though, and Bette (but not Joan) was nominated for an Academy Award. Yet it was Joan who stood on the Oscar stage that year, thanks to a deal she'd made with all of Bette's competitors to accept their awards on their behalf if they won. An attempt at another film pairing failed when Crawford quit. Years later, when asked for a comment following Joan's 1977 death, Bette got in the last, brutal words. "You should never say bad things about the dead, you should only say good. Joan Crawford is dead. Good." Ouch.'

Joan did some strange horror films and thrillers at the end of her career. An old trooper to the end, she somehow managed to maintain her poise and dignity in these movies. Her last film was the 1970 British horror film Trog. In the film a troglodyte (and I'm not making this up) is found in a cave and Joan's doctor, who thinks it might be a missing link, must try and understand and domestic it. Or something like that. The BFI later said of Trog - 'One of the most ludicrous, touching, mind-boggling star vehicles ever. Joan Crawford, desperate for a job, teams up with director Freddie Francis(!) and an actor in a pitiful monkey mask for a sci-fi howler like no other.'

Joan had somewhat better luck on television around this time when she was in a segment of the Rod Serling hosted anthology show Night Gallery titled Eyes. Eyes was directed by a young unknown director named Steven Spielberg (wonder what happened to him in the end?) and stars Joan as Miss Claudia Menlo, a wealthy and influential woman who has been blind since birth. Art lover Menlo hears about an extraordinary new operation that will enable her to see and becomes obsessed with undertaking the procedure - even if trials have suggested the effects might not be permanent but only temporary. Even a few hours to look at art would make it worth everything and anything to her.

She needs two things to undertake the operation though. A donor willing to part with their eyes and eyesight and a doctor who is prepared to carry out the operation. For the first part of the equation, Meno finds what appears to be a willing donor in the desperate debt ridden Sidney Resnick (Tom Bosley) but getting hold of a doctor who is prepared to be a part of this might be more difficult. Menlo will have to be persuasive and ruthless where a certain Dr Heatherton (Barry Sullivan) is concerned.

Eyes never quite strikes a bullseye but but Crawford is excellent (one imagines it must have been slightly daunting for the young Spielberg to be adapting a Rod Serling script and have Joan Crawford as his star) and Happy Days actor Tom Bosley (in a role Serling had intended for Twilight Zone regular Jack Klugman) is great as the hopelessly debt mired blue collar loser so desperate he is willing to lose his sight just to clear his money problems.

Serling doesn't sweep this character under the carpet. Quite the contrary. He gives Bosley a dialogue scene that makes us feel for his plight and the awful scenario Resnick now views as unavoidable. You can see that Spielberg is really doing his best to put his stamp on the episode, jazz it up and impress. He deploys unusual camera angles and wide shots and even shoots Crawford through a glittering chandelier at one point. There is a decent suspenseful finish too and while never quite a classic Night Gallery story, Eyes is always highly competent and interesting.

By 1974, Joan Crawford had become a recluse after seeing some unflattering photographs of herself in the newspaper. She decided that she'd rather people remembered her as she was in her Hollywood heyday rather than how she looked now. Joan lived in a New York apartment located at 150 E. 69th Street. She's sold her Hollywood mansion and moved to the Big Apple. There was a bit of Howard Hughes in Joan - and not just in the need for privacy. It is said that her main hobby was scrubbing her apartment clean because she was obsessed with germs and cleanliness. Joan was apparently also fond of sitting up all night to catch television screenings of her old movies.

By 1977 she had been bedridden for months and was being looked after by two ladies. Joan had apparently converted to Christian Science in 1975 and didn't want to see a doctor. She had become very thin and it seemed as though she was preparing herself to die. The end came on Tuesday May 10, 1977. No one actually knew how old she was. She was presumed to be 69 but could have been older. By the time of her death, Joan was only on speaking terms with her twin daughters, Cathy and Cindy. Her other children, Christopher and Christina, were estranged and cut out of the will. Joan Crawford had a Unitarian funeral service in New York City and was cremated. There weren't actually many Hollywood stars at Joan's funeral but there was a star studded turn out for a tribute to Joan staged in Beverly Hills a month later. To many people in Hollywood the death of Joan Crawford was the end of a golden era.

In 1978, Christina Crawford, the adopted daughter of Joan Crawford, wrote a memoir about her late mother titled Mommie Dearest that shocked Hollywood. Christina alleged that Joan Crawford was a sadistic alcoholic who treated her children as if they were prisoners and would fly into wild rages at the drop of a hat. Among the claims made in the book were that Joan Crawford would drunkenly wake her children in the middle of the night and force them to clean the house, once nearly killed Christina when she throttled her, shredded Christina's most beloved dress into rags and then made her wear it to humiliate her, trussed her children up at night so they couldn't move, and once starved Christina for days when she refused to eat a steak at dinner.

Christina also seemed to suggest that Joan Crawford might have killed her fourth husband! The book was turned into a memorably camp and over the top 1981 film with Faye Dunaway (Christina had nothing to do with the film and called it 'grotesque) but was it a work of fact or fiction? Critics of the book included Joan Crawford's two younger children, Cindy and Cathy, who stated categorically many times that they did not witness or experience any of the events that were described in the book. Joan Crawford's secretary also said she had never witnessed any of the abuse alleged by Christina.

Showbusiness figures like Van Johnson, Cesar Romero, Bob Hope, Barbara Stanwyck, Sydney Guilaroff, Ann Blyth, Gary Gray, Myrna Loy, and Douglas Fairbanks Jr. (Crawford's first husband), also disputed the depiction of Joan Crawford in Mommie Dearest. Those who supported Christina though included her adopted brother Christopher and showbusiness figures like Helen Hayes, James MacArthur, June Allyson, Rex Reed, and Betty Hutton. Hutton said she used to used to encourage her children to engage with and play with Joan Crawford's children so they would get a respite from their mother. Eve Arden was another person in showbusiness who believed Christina and felt that Joan Crawford was an alcoholic prone to erratic mood swings.

Joan Crawford did not live to read Mommie Dearest - although she is said to have known that Christina was writing a memoir about her childhood. It is said that Joan Crawford, not long before she died, attempted to reconnect with her estranged daughter but nothing came of this. Christina is not convinced that her's mother's attempt at a reconciliation was genuine. She is still adamant too that Mommie Dearest is the truth and a sobering tale of abuse, alcoholism, and Borderline personality disorder.

DOROTHY DELL

Dorothy Dell was born in Hattiesburg, Mississippi, in 1915. Dell won a lot of beauty pageants as a youngster and was also Miss New Orleans. Her family were quite well off and had connections to the entertainment industry. Dorothy had a wonderful singing voice and decided to go into vaudeville (she apparently did this because it would allow her mother to tag along). She was also friends with Dorothy Lamour. Dell was soon noticed on the stage by an agent and asked to join the Ziegfeld Follies on Broadway. She was romantically linked to the singer Russ Columbo in the media and this saw her profile rocket thanks to gossip columns.

Dorothy had all the makings of a big star in that she was hip and very in vogue with her short blonde hair. She could not only sing but act too. A lot of aspiring stars of this era were wooden when they actually got to speak on screen but Dell was something of a natural. You could say she was a bit like a younger more wholesome version of Thelma Todd. In 1933, after a successful screen test, Dorothy Dell was signed by Paramount and given a film contract. She made her debut (beyond bit parts) in the 1934 film Wharf Angel.

In the film Warf Angel, Dorothy played Toy, a woman who works in a saloon. Victor McLaglen (a former boxer who once had an exhibition fight with Jack Johnson) was the lead. Dorothy stole the picture from under everyone's noses with her rendition of Down Home. Dorothy got rave reviews for Wharf Angel and the studio were very confident they could turn her into a huge star. In her next film Little Miss Marker, Dorothy was cast with the biggest child star in Hollywood history - Shirly Temple. Temple was loaned to Paramount by Fox for this film. It was Shirly's mother who did the deal.

Little Miss Marker is about "Marky" (Shirley Temple), a little girl who ends up being raised by gangsters after her father uses her as collateral in a wager and then commits suicide when he loses the bet! As you might imagine from the plot, this was a pre-code film. Despite the plot though it's a fairly light-hearted film with plenty of comedy. Dorothy Dell plays the wonderfully named Bangles Carson in the film. Bangles is a gangster's moll and ends up forming a sort of mother/daughter bond with young Marky.

Shirley Temple became very close to Dorothy Dell during the making of Little Miss Marker. Sometimes they had to do several takes of a scene because Shirley Temple and Dorothy would make each other laugh so much. The scene where Temple as Marky goes into a strop and refuses food was a nightmare to shoot in particular because Dorothy kept laughing. Paramount had Shirley Temple on a two picture contract loan and planned to put her in another film with Dorothy Dell. Alas, these plans would never happen in the end.

Dorothy's next film was a comedy called Shoot the Works in which she played a singer called Lily. After watching a preview of the film, Dorothy agreed to go for a trip with a 38 year-old surgeon named Carl Wagner. Wagner was taking Dorothy to meet his mother. They had become close because Dr Wagner had successfully treated Dorothy's mother for an illness not long ago. Wagner told Dorothy that she needed a break from the studio and the trip would be good. Dorothy was supposed to go back and shoot a few more final scenes for Shoot the Works after her break.

Despite the attentions of Dr Wagner, they were apparently just friends. Dorothy was actually engaged to a man named Nat Carson. Carson was in London and had proposed to Dorothy a week before. After meeting Dr Wagner's mother, Dorothy and Dr Wagner went to a celebrity party and a good time. After this they headed back to Beverley Hills (where Dorothy lived with her parents and younger sister) but tragedy struck when the car hit a telephone pole and collided with a tree and a boulder.

Wagner had been driving at around 70 mph and lost control. He died of his injuries several hours later. As for Dorothy Dell, she was killed instantly. She was just nineteen years-old. Dorothy was judged to have died from a skull fracture. The crash took place around 2am. The car was completely mangled in the crash so Dorothy and Dr Wagner had little chance of surviving. It was just an awful tragic accident in which Dr Wagner completely lost control of the car.

Dorothy Dell's death was a great tragedy not just for her friends and family but also for Hollywood because her career had only just begun. She had the acting chops and singing voice to be a genuine star and although she was young she wasn't reliant on youthful looks because she looked very mature onscreen for her age. Nat Carson, who was due to marry Dorothy, decided to stay in London when he heard the news. He was devastated. Carson had been planning a six month Honeymoon break with Dorothy because he thought she needed a good rest from movies.

Another person who was absolutely devastated by Dorothy's death was Shirley Temple. There is a Hollywood legend, most likely a myth, that Shirley was only told of Dorothy's death just before shooting a crying scene so that her tears would be genuine. Whether true or not, Shirley did cry real tears for Dorothy in private. On working with Dorothy Dell, Temple said - "I felt treated as an equal. Time and again during the film she turned out to be a splendid foil for my energy and exuberance. My special affection for her was based on this positive attitude, one which made me feel inches taller than I was."

At a memorial service for Dorothy, some of her famous friends in showbusiness sang in tribute. Dorothy was laid to rest at Metairie Cemetery in southeastern Louisiana. For two years after her death fan mail for Dorothy continued to pour into the studio mailbox. Dorothy Dell has just four entries on her IMDB page. Had she not been taken so soon it's safe to say that her IMDB page would have been considerable in the end.

DUSTIN DIAMOND

Dustin Diamond was born in San Jose, California in 1977. He was a child actor and had roles in things like The Wonder Years and The Munsters Today. It was though his role as Samuel 'Screech' Powers on Saved by the Bell and its endless spin-offs which catapulted him to fame at a young age. Screech had a voice which could grate cheese at a hundred yards - hence his name. Saved by the Bell launched the careers of Elizabeth Berkley, Tiffani Thiessen, Mark-Paul Gosselaar, and Mario Lopez. While they were - to varying degrees - the cool and beautiful kids, Dustin was strictly the comic relief.

Diamond was definitely odd - even as a kid - but that was ok. In a strange way it was sort of comforting to have a kid like this on a show where people are usually cast for how they look. Dustin made kids feel like it was alright to be a bit different and eccentric and he threw himself into the part of Screech with scenery chewing enthusiasm. Dustin played Screech in numerous Saved by the Bell spin-offs into his twenties. In fact, he was even in Good Morning, Miss Bliss too - which retrospectively became known as Saved by the Bell: The Junior High Years. If you mention Saved by the Bell to people of a certain age you can guarantee that the first image that will then come into their head is Samuel 'Screech' Powers. Screech was a geeky nerd with a shock mop of obstreperous black hair. One might even argue that the character was rather ahead of his time and anticipated things like The Big Bang Theory.

Once the Saved by the Bell franchise finally spluttered (for now at least) to a halt, Diamond found that life in Hollywood was no bed of roses. He had of course - inevitably - been typecast as Screech so found it difficult to get roles in anything else. As soon as you see Dustin Diamond you think Screech. Just as Gary Coleman was never going to escape from the shadow of Arnold Jackson, Dustin Diamond was never realistically going to thesp his way out of the Screech legacy. The solution to this problem would have been for him to just play Screech forever but, as we shall see, this was rather taken out out of his hands in the end.

It's fair to say that the other cast members in Saved by the Bell did better than Dustin in their careers. Mark-Paul Gosselaar never really became a star but he was in some movies and the co-lead in NYPD Blue. Tiffani Thiessen never became a big star either but she worked all the time and was in a Woody Allen film. Mario Lopez has also worked endlessly and became a successful television presenter. Elizabeth Berkley NEARLY became a star when she was cast in the Paul Verhoven film Showgirls but we all know what happened there. Still, her career was none too shabby after that and she has appeared in many big TV shows and an Oliver Stone film.

Which brings us right back to Dustin Diamond. Dustin ended up mostly earning his living through reality television. He was, thanks to Screech, a cultish comic sort of celebrity and so was always in demand to make cameos as himself in movies (it must have irked Dustin somewhat that he was asked to play Dustin Diamond but never actually a new character) or do a reality show. He even appeared on the British version of Celebrity Big Brother. Just in case you were curious, Dustin was evicted from the Big Brother house on day fifteen. The winner that year was Charlotte Crosby (whoever she is when she's at home). Other celebrities in the house included the former football manager Ron Atkinson, Coronation Street star Bruce Jones, and rentagob radio and television personality Carol McGiffin. The baffled Dustin didn't have the faintest idea who any of these people were.

In 2006, Dustin Diamond was - in a rarity for him - in the headlines when a sex tape of him emerged. Screech in a sex tape? It was such a bizarre story that entertainment sites couldn't help but be fascinated. It did rather smack of a desperate attempt by Dustin at gaining some publicity for a flagging career and was rather tawdry given his fame as a children's television icon. Diamond would later say that the tape was a hoax and he wasn't even really in it. Whether this was true or merely deflection is hard to say with certainty. He did claim though that during his time on Saved by the Bell he slept with 2,000 women. Given that he was only 21 when the last show (that he was involved with anyway) ended this would appear to be a dubious claim. It's hard to imagine Dustin as some teenage version of Warren Beatty sleeping with every person in Los Angeles.

Dustin was certainly a colourful character in real life. He was a karate black-belt and loved wrestling so much he even got in the ring himself. He was also in a metal band. By all accounts Dustin was an easygoing sort of person who just wanted to have a good time. In 2009, Diamond released a book called Behind the Bell which was a warts and all account of life on the set of Saved by the Bell. His participation in this book turned out to be a big mistake. The book was highly critical of Dustin's co-stars on Saved by the Bell. It depicted them as pill popping sex maniacs with out of control egos. It was a generally unflattering portrait to say the least.

Dustin would later, in a desperate damage limitation exercise, claim that the book was ghostwritten by someone who took his interviews completely out of context and embellished them for entertainment. Well, maybe that was truth but the damage had been done. Dustin was the Screech Who Cried Wolf at this point. It was hard to know when - if ever - he was telling the truth. Dustin Diamond was married to Jennifer Misner from 2009 until their separation in 2013. Oddly though there was apparently no legal evidence that they were officially married. In a way that was typical Dustin Diamond. He was like a budget version of Andy Kaufman.

2013 was eventful for Dustin because he was also declared bankrupt in this year. The money from his acting career as a child and teenager was long gone. This was a classic trope in Hollywood. Dustin was essentially a child star and his salad days were over. Also in 2013, Dustin gave an interview to his former Saved by the Bell co-star Mario Lopez and apologised for Behind the Bell. Dustin, rather touchingly, said he hadn't seen Elizabeth Berkley, Tiffani Thiessen, or Mark-Paul Gosselaar since the last show ended all those years ago. He said he just wanted to give them a hug and congratulate them on the work they had done.

In 2014, Dustin Diamond was arrested in Wisconsin after he pulled out a knife during an altercation in a bar. He was convicted of two misdemeanors: carrying a concealed weapon and disorderly conduct. Diamond served three months in prison for his offences. Dustin Diamond's acting career had pretty much vanished without trace by this point. By now Diamond was definitely paying the price too for Behind the Bell. The original Saved by the Bell cast did a shoot for

People Magazine in 2009 but Dustin was not asked to take part. In 2015 some of the cast did a Saved by the Bell skit on The Tonight Show but once again Dustin Diamond was absent. It must have been very hurtful for him to have been airbrushed out of something that he put more time into than anyone. The original Saved by the Bell stars had cancelled Dustin Diamond.

In 2020, Saved by the Bell was revived as a sitcom on Peacock. It was a sort of Saved By the Bell: The Next Generation and all the original cast members were involved. Well, all except one person. You can probably guess who that was. Dustin Diamond expressed his disappointment (he argued, not unreasonably, that you can't have a Saved by the Bell reunion without Screech!) at being left out and although the producers made vague comments about the 'door being open' for him it was obvious that no one on the show wanted anything to do with Dustin after Behind the Bell.

At the end of January in 2021, it was reported in the media that Dustin Diamond had been diagnosed with stage 4 lung cancer. Believe it or not some people actually suspected Diamond of staging another publicity stunt with this story and wondered if it was even true. Sadly, it was all true. Diamond died from the disease in Florida on February 1, 2021, at the young age of 44. Diagnosis to death had taken two weeks. It seemed rather unfair that Dustin Diamond had lost his life to lung cancer when he didn't even smoke. "Dustin did not suffer," said his agent. "He did not have to lie submerged in pain. For that, we are grateful." Dustin Diamond (like most of us) hated going to the doctor and had put off getting a check-up even when he began to suspect he was ill. By the time he did get diagnosed it was too late.

Elizabeth Berkley, Tiffani Thiessen, and Mark-Paul Gosselaar all posted warm tributes to Dustin Diamond on social media when he died. To read their tributes you'd think they'd all been best pals with him. One might suggest this was somewhat hypocritical as they had avoided him like the plague when he was alive and he was never invited to the Saved by the Bell nostalgia skits and photo ops they arranged. The thing that must have hurt Dustin most of all was being snubbed on the Saved by the Bell reunion show. He would have loved to have gone full circle and played an adult Screech. Dustin had been planning to marry a woman he met on Facebook at the time of his death. Alas, all these plans would never transpire now. Dustin didn't want a grave and asked to be cremated. It is believed that the ashes were given to his father.

BOBBY DRISCOLL

Bobby Driscoll was born in Cedar Rapids, Iowa in 1937. Driscoll's father was an insulation salesman and his mother was a former teacher. Because Mr Driscoll was in quite poor health due to bad lungs they moved to California to be in a warmer place. Bobby was a cute kid and his parents were encouraged to put him forward for some child acting. Bobby ended up auditioning for a small part in a film called Lost Angel and bagged the role. A slew of other acting parts soon followed but it was for his association with Walt Disney that he would be best remembered for.

Driscoll was the first child actor ever to be given a contract by Disney. Walt loved Bobby Driscoll and said the boy reminded him of himself at that age. Bobby appeared in Song of the South, So Dear To My Heart, and Treasure Island. He also won two Juvenile academy awards. We tend to think that child actors in Old Hollywood were a trifle wooden and limited compared to child actors today but Bobby Driscoll was the real deal. This kid could genuinely act. He was even loaned to other studios by Disney to make films for them.

1953 was the peak of Bobby's career as he was both the voice and the model for Disney's animated Peter Pan film. He attended the Hollywood Professional School at 5400 Hollywood Blvd and was making $50,000 a year (which was a lot of money back then). His income was supplemented by his duties supplying voices for cartoons. He would even play Peter Pan in live appearances for Disney. Though he had no way of knowing it at the time, Bobby had now passed the high water mark of his career. He was still a teenager but it would be downhill from here on in. There have been child actors who went on to have long and successful careers (look at Natalie Portman and Christian Bale for example) but Bobby Driscoll was not destined to be one of them. Some of this was his fault and some of it wasn't.

Bobby Driscoll's problems began when Disney terminated his contract a few weeks before Peter Pan opened. Why was he let go? It was simple. Bobby Driscoll was getting older. He was hitting puberty and now had acne. They had no use for him anymore. There were new younger fresh faced kids to take his place. Despite his obvious talent as an actor, Bobby Driscoll never managed to get back to the heights he had scaled in his early days in Hollywood. His career thereafter was a long decline into relative obscurity.

Legend has it that Howard Hughes through his purchase of RKO took control of Disney and decided to get rid of the Disney kids because he hated them. There is a story that Bobby Driscoll and his family only found out about this when they drove to the Disney studio and were denied permission to enter through the gate. That was brutal if true. It must have felt like being locked out of your own home. Bobby was 16 now though and he must have known that his Disney kid days were on borrowed time anyway.

Bobby continued to work for a time but instead of big Disney pictures he was now employed in (long forgotten) television anthology shows and in radio serials. He was taken out of the Hollywood school where all the entertainment industry kids went and sent to a normal school. Bobby found this terrifying. He was a fish out of water in the new school because he had nothing in common with ordinary kids and teenagers. What made it worse was that other pupils would mock him for his Disney background.

Bobby began to go off the rails and started taking drugs. Unfortunately, Bobby, unlike most teenagers his age, had plenty of money to buy whatever drugs he wanted. He even began injecting heroin. Though he was eventually sent back to the Hollywood school to finish his studies by now it was too late. He had already begun to spiral into narcotic dependency. In 1956, Bobby was arrested for possession of heroin but the charge was dismissed. As you can imagine, the media had a field day. Peter Pan arrested!

A few years later Bobby eloped to Mexico to get married and had some children but the marriage did not last very long. The work he was picking up now was strictly television work - and he was lucky to get that. He did himself no favours when he barely escaped an assault rap for hitting someone with a pistol while washing his car. One of his last roles was in the western show Rawhide. In 1961, he was sentenced as a drug addict and imprisoned at the Narcotic Rehabilitation Center of the California Institution for Men in Chino, California. It wasn't just drug use that made up Bobby's infractions. He had also been involved in burglary and forging cheques.

Upon his release the following year, Bobby Driscoll found himself to be unemployable. Talk about rags to riches. Not only did he now have a criminal record but the drug use had taken its toll. He had missing teeth, bad hygiene, and just hadn't been looking after himself. In less than ten years he had gone from Disney's golden boy to a drug addled has been. "I have found that memories are not very useful," said Bobby. "I was carried on a silver platter—and then dumped into the garbage."

It is certainly true that Bobby was treated harshly by Hollywood but then he didn't help matters by turning to drugs. A lot of former child stars have got into drugs. The general theory is that they are trying to somehow replicate the high of the fame and adulation they used to have as children. The loss of that fame has created a hole which they attempt to fill through drugs. Bobby was now broke. To cap it all he'd lost his Oscars in a house fire. Bobby must have felt like someone had put a curse on him.

Bobby ended up in New York where, believe it or not, he became a friend of Andy Warhol. Bobby was a talented artist by all accounts too in this period. Sadly though, Bobby was not able to pull his life out of the rubble and come up with a third act. On March 30, 1968, two children were exploring an abandoned building in the East Village and found Bobby's dead body. He was laying on a cot with some empty beer bottles. He was just 31 years-old. Though no drugs were found in his system, drugs had obviously wrecked Bobby's health in the previous years. The autopsy found he'd died of occlusive coronary arteriosclerosis. Obstructive coronary artery disease is the gradual narrowing or closing of arteries that supply the heart with blood.

Here now is the saddest part of the Bobby Driscoll story. He was, strangely given his criminal record, not identified by the police because he had no ID. No one came forward to claim him either. Bobby was therefore buried on Hart Island - which was used as the burial place of the unknown. In short, a paupers' grave. Bobby's parents hadn't seen him for a long time and had no idea he was dead. They eventually asked Disney for help in tracking Bobby down and fingerprints were used to discover that Bobby had died in New York and been buried on Hart Island. Bobby's remains are still there - although his name was later added to his father's grave.

No one actually knows where exactly on the island Bobby is buried - which seems a shame as he surely deserved some sort of monument. Melinda Hunt of The Hart Island Project (which helps people find loved ones who were buried on Hart Island) said though - "My feeling is that it's not a shameful place to be buried. It's a really, really beautiful location. There are herds of deer, these red raccoons, and a whole bird sanctuary. So for Bobby Driscoll, it's the perfect place to be buried. It's just like Never Never Land." Bobby Driscoll was a kid who had everything and ended up with nothing. His legacy though through Disney and films like The Window will live on forever.

ANDRES ESCOBAR

Andrés Escobar was born in Medellín, Colombia in 1967. Escobar was a talented footballer from a young age and was most associated with his local club Atlético Nacional - for whom he made over 200 appearances in two spells. Escobar also played for BSC Young Boys in Switzerland. Escobar was a central defender nicknamed The Gentleman because of his unflappable style of play and clean tackling. He made his debut the Colombian national team in 1988 and won 51 caps. Were it not for his untimely demise he would have won many more. Escobar's father was a banker who created a scheme where youngsters could play football rather than get into trouble on the streets. Andrés Escobar won a lot of praise in Columbia himself too for the way that he promoted the country and tried to improve its image.

Andrés Escobar's fate, though no one could have known it, was probably sealed by Columbia qualifying for the 1994 World Cup in the United States. Columbia had qualified in impressive fashion and many pundits believed they had a good chance of going a long way in the tournament. Columbia had some genuine stars in their team like Faustino Asprilla and Carlos Valderrama so a lot was expected of them. Naturally a lot of this expectation resided in Columbia. Strangely, Andrés Escobar was not picked for the qualifying matches but he did make the World Cup squad. In hindsight, it's a shame he didn't miss out on selection. That way he might still be alive today.

Andrés Escobar played in all three of Columbia's matches in the World Cup. They had a disastrous start when they lost 3-1 to a strong Romania team. This made their second match, against the host nation the United States, all the more crucial. If you lose your first two matches in the World Cup you are more likely than not toast. Once again though, Columbia came up short - losing 2-1. Andrés Escobar's 35th minute own goal was a big factor in the match. The USA then scored a second goal just after half-time and Columbia had a mountain to climb. They only scored in the 90th minute - which was far too late to affect the match.

Columbia won their last match 2-0 against Switzerland but it was too late. They finished bottom of their group and crashed out of the tournament. There was a lot of disappointment in Columbia at their team's early exit. The national side had flopped on the big stage. Still, it's only a game isn't it? It isn't the end of the world. Or shouldn't be at any rate. After the early exit of the Columbian national team, Escobar went back home (he had been advised to lay low after the own goal but Andrés Escobar insisted that he should not hide from his own people). About five days later he was with some friends in the El Poblado neighbourhood in Medellín. It was here that fate fashioned a cruel and unexpected twist.

Escobar and his friends went to a nightclub and much later, around 3am, Escobar sat alone in his car in the car park. As he sat there three men approached the car and words were exchanged. Escobar was then shot six times and bled to death before he could be treated in hospital. He was 27 years-old. The men are said to have shouted 'Goal!' each time they shot him. The suggestion in the media at the time was that Escobar had been shot in a bizarre sort of 'revenge anger' incident for his own goal in the World Cup. That wasn't quite accurate though, at least according to the evidence.

A man named Humberto Castro Muñoz was arrested for the murder of Andrés Escobar. Muñoz was muscle for a drug cartel. In short, a dangerous criminal. His accomplices were not charged with anything. Muñoz was also a driver for Santiago Gallon. Santiago Gallon was a Colombian drug trafficker and a leader of the Gallon gang. The general theory is that Santiago Gallon lost a lot of money betting on Columbia in the World Cup and so ordered that Andrés Escobar should be killed in revenge for his own goal. What gave this theory some credence is that Humberto Castro Muñoz was sentenced to 43 years in prison for the murder but got let out after about 10 years. The inference is that Santiago Gallon used bribes or his influence to get Muñoz out of his prison sentence early. The truth is hard to verify for sure.

What made this murder all even more tragic is that Andrés Escobar, at the time of his death, was due to marry a woman named Pamela Cascardo. This marriage would never happen now. 120,000 people turned out for Andrés Escobar's funeral and a statue of him was created in his home town. At the time of his death it is said that he had an offer to play for A.C Milan in Italy. He still had much to offer the football world and most of his life was still ahead of him but sadly an inexplicably senseless and violent murder put an end to the exceptional life of Andrés Escobar. A few days after the murder of Andrés Escobar, the BBC had to offer an apology when their World Cup pundit Alan Hansen suggested an Argentian defender 'should be shot' for making a bad mistake in a game. Talk about putting your foot in your mouth.

JUSTIN FASHANU

Justinus Soni "Justin" Fashanu was born in London in 1961. Justin was the son of a Nigerian barrister and a Guyanese nurse. When his parents split up, Justin and his brother John were fostered and brought up by a white couple in Norfolk. Justin and John said it wasn't easy growing up in Norfolk because they often felt like the only two black kids in the entire area. Justin was an awesome boxer as a teenager by all accounts but he was also a natural when it came to football. While playing for his school team, Justin was scouted by his local club Norwich City and signed as an apprentice. Justin played as a striker. He was tall and fast and looked to have all the attributes necessary to go right to the top.

Justin made his league debut for Norwich City in 1978. In his three year spell at the club Justin scored 40 goals in 103 games - which is an impressive return for someone so young. He also won 11 caps for the England under 21 team - scoring five times. Justin was said to be rather disappointed though that he didn't get a call up to the full England squad. More established players like Paul Mariner, Tony Woodcock, Trevor Francis, and Kevin Keegan were ahead of Fashanu at this time in the international pecking order so he never got that elusive call up. Justin famously won the Goal of the Season award in 1980 for his spectacular goal against Liverpool.

Justin's brother John was at Norwich City with him but John decided to move on to another team because he felt like he was in Justin's shadow. John said that he felt like Justin never helped him at Norwich City as much as he'd wanted and so this seemed to create a distance between the brothers which was never really healed. The two brothers could not have been more different. Justin was shy (though outspoken) and sensitive and was all about grace as a player. John was tough and confident and was an old fashioned target man who could use his strength to hold off defenders. Justin and John were just very different people.

Despite the goals Justin was banging in for them, Norwich City were struggling as a team and it was evident that Justin was going to move to a bigger club sooner or later. He had outgrown Norwich City and although they were going to miss Justin as a player Norwich knew that his departure would be sweetened with a huge transfer fee. In 1981, Justin signed for Nottingham Forest in a deal that made him Britain's first one million pound black footballer. The actual fee was around £1.6 million - which was huge money to spend on a player in 1981. Forest were confident though that they were buying the most exciting young striker in the country and that Justin was a great investment in the future of their team. Sadly though, this transfer did not turn out very well in the end for either Justin or fans of Nottingham Forest.

Forest, under their legendary, brilliant, and highly eccentric manager Brian Clough, had just won back to back European Cups. Forest were now looking to freshen up their team and build for the future. Justin was essentially bought by Forest as a replacement for Trevor Francis (who scored the winning goal for Forest in the 1979 European Cup Final). Francis was sold to Manchester City by Forest in 1981. It was at Nottingham Forest that Justin's highly promising football career began to hit the buffers. Justin never really managed to get back on track after his experience with Nottingham Forest. It all went wrong very quickly.

Justin was secretly gay. Given the tribal, old-fashioned, and politically incorrect nature of the football world it was very difficult for Justin to be a gay man and a footballer. Even today hardly any footballers have come out as gay for fear of the damage it might do to their career or the stick they might get from the crowds. It was even worse back in 1981. Much worse. A number of sports people from a range of sports today are openly gay and it's no big deal. Sadly though, for whatever reason, men's football seems to be the outlier when it comes to tolerance. There is just something about the football world which makes footballers very reluctant to come out.

Justin had been visiting a gay club in the Nottingham area and word of this got back to Brian Clough. In those days footballers were expected to drink beer with their teammates and then go home to their wives. The notion of a gay footballer was a completely alien concept. Brian Clough was not only annoyed but genuinely perplexed when he found out that Justin Fashanu seemed to be gay. Clough was an old fashioned man who clearly didn't like the idea that one of his players was gay. Legend has it that Clough asked Justin in front of the whole team if he was gay. It was a humiliating approach and would not be tolerated today.

Justin was dropped like a stone by Clough and Forest. He was banned from training with the first team (Clough is alleged to have called the police when Justin defied the ban and turned up to training) and then sent on loan to Southampton. Brian Clough wanted Justin out of Nottingham Forest as fast as possible. In December 1982, Justin was sold to Notts County - who were Forest's Nottingham rivals. The fee was £100,000. Forest had taken a massive financial loss on Fashanu with this deal but it illustrated how desperate Clough was to get rid of him. Justin's salary at Notts County was half what it had been at Forest but he didn't care. He was simply relieved to go somewhere where the manager and club made him feel welcome.

Justin at least had a happier time at Notts County, scoring over 20 goals in three seasons at the club. The staff at Notts County really liked Justin and they said he was great at taking part in community activities in the local area. However, the promise he had displayed as a youngster was never really fufilled. Justin actually retired in 1986 due to injury but then made a seemingly endless series of comebacks. He moved to Brighton next but a bad injury more or less ended his career at the highest level.

There were occasionally flashes his old form and occasionally he'd get one more chance at the big time (like a spell at Manchester City and a trial for at Newcastle) but it never amounted to regular top flight football anywhere. Justin now became a wandering nomad of a footballer. He played in the United States, Canada, Scotland, non league football, for other English clubs. He went all over the place.

In 1990, Justin Fashanu came out as gay in an interview for The Sun newspaper. At the time no footballer had ever come out before. The reaction was depressingly spiteful and cold. Justin received terrible abuse from crowds and his teammates would make crude jokes. Worst of all was the fact that his brother John also seemed to disown him. The articulate and charismatic John Fashanu probably became best known for his stint hosting the 90s ITV game show Gladiators.

In his playing days, John Fashanu was a big physical striker who was good in the air and handy with his elbows (as Gary Mabbutt's eye socket will testify). John Fashunu was not exactly mobile but he was effective if you played a particular brand of football. He was one of those strikers who could hold the ball up and be a complete nuisance when it came to corners and free kicks. John Fashanu scored 107 goals in 276 appearances at Wimbledon and this was enough to earn him a couple of England caps in 1989.

John Fashanu was one of football's hard men' and he was clearly unhappy when stories filtered out that his brother was gay. John made some rather unfortunate comments about his brother Justin coming out. John said that Justin was an outcast. He also suggested that Justin wasn't even gay and was just doing it for some attention. It later came to light that John had offered Justin money to keep quiet about being gay.

The Sun article alleged Justin had an affair with a Tory member of parliament. Justin later sold a story to The Sunday People in which he claimed he'd slept with two cabinet ministers. When the police contacted Justin in the wake of the strange death of Stephen Milligan (a Tory politician we shall discuss later in this book) to ask if he knew anything about Milligan's private life, Justin had to confess that he'd made all this stuff up.

A big factor in Justin selling stories to the tabloids was obviously money but also because Justin seemed to crave the limelight. The days when he made headlines on the football pitch were long gone. Justin said he suffered a 'backlash' when he came out as gay. Back on the field, Justin had a decent spell at Torquay United and even served as their assistant manager but his days at the top were long gone.

While Justin was at Torquay United, he sold a bizarre story to the tabloids in which he claimed he was having an affair with the actress Julie Goodyear - an older woman who famously played the brassy barmaid Bet Lynch in the soap opera Coronation Street. The article was (memorably) titled My Bet on the Side. Julie Goodyear would later say that she was just friends with Justin. The story of them having an affair was fictitious. Justin was now pretending he was bisexual for some reason. There is a theory that Justin got into religion for a time in this period and it messed his head up somewhat.

Justin's career limped onto until 1997. His last port of call was New Zealand. He'd clocked up more miles than Michael Palin by the time he hung up his football boots for the last time. After his retirement, Justin moved to the United States and took up a coaching position with Maryland Mania. In March 1998, a teenager claimed that Justin had sexually assaulted him as he slept after a night of drinking. Gay sex was actually illegal in Maryland at the time.

Police officers visited Justin's apartment to question him. They later returned with a warrant to arrest him on charges of second-degree sexual assault, first-degree assault, and second-degree assault. Justin wasn't there though. He had gone back to England without telling anyone. On May the 3rd, Justin was found dead in a garage in Shoreditch. He had hung himself at the age of 37. In his suicide note Justin said he was innocent of the sexual assault but feared he wouldn't get a fair hearing because he was gay. In order to save his family from any embarrassment he had decided to take his own life.

He had written - 'Being gay and a personality is so hard, but everybody has it hard at the moment, so I can't complain about that. I want to say I didn't sexually assault the young boy. He willingly had sex with me and then the next day asked for money. When I said no, he said 'you wait and see.' If that is the case, I hear you say, why did I run? Well, justice isn't always fair. I felt I wouldn't get a fair trial because of my homosexuality.'

An inquest into Justin's death suggested that the police in the United States would have asked for him to be extradited had it become public where he was. If found guilty Justin could have been looking at 20 years in prison. Justin's friends and family did not believe the charges against him were fair. Justin, as his note said, claimed it was a consensual encounter. Justin Fashanu was cremated after a service at the City of London Cemetery and Crematorium. John Fashanu and people from the world of football attended. President Nelson Mandela sent a message of condolence.

John Fashanu later expressed regret at the way he had handled his brother's sexuality. "If anyone was to blame for what happened it was me. I shunned my brother. If I was like that with him, what was everyone else like? I feel a bit cross with myself that I didn't see these challenges Justin was having. A little bit more understanding and a little bit more softness could've changed a lot of things.

Whether you like him or you don't like him, or you love him or you hate him, Justin Fashanu is a legend."

The Justin Fashanu Foundation now campaigns to end homophobia in football and supports a number of players unable to come out publicly as gay. Justin's niece Amal Fashanu, who made an award winning documentary about her late uncle in 2017, said - "He was picked on because of his sexuality, made to feel inferior, different, wrong. He was a lost soul, but even then his precedent secretly gave a lot of people hope. I get messages about what an inspiration he was from all around the world, all the time. It needed someone like Justin to come along who had no fear of repercussions and wasn't prepared to live his life as lie."

FRITZ HAARMANN

Fritz Haarmann was born in Hanover, Germany in 1879. In true crime circles he is known as The Vampire of Hanover for reasons we'll get to very soon. Haarmann was an unhappy child (what else is new when it comes to serial killers?) and seemed to have a lifelong bitterness at his father. He suffered seizures when he was a boy and it is speculated that these might have left some lasting damage that impaired his mental health. He went to a military academy (in those days Germany was obviously a more militaristic nation) but was kicked out because they didn't think he was healthy enough to make a good student or potential soldier.

After this, Haarmann got married (although he was secretly gay) and picked up some work at a shipping docks. Money was still tight though and he became a petty thief - which earned him a short spell in prison. It was after his release from prison that Haarmann seemed to completely snap and become a deranged serial killer. His victims were the usual serial killer targets. Prostitutes, runaways, homeless people. All of his victims were boys or men. Haarmann would lure the victims back to his home with promises of food and drink. When they were vulnerable he would bite them in the throat in savage fashion. He referred to this as a 'love bite'.

If this 'love bite' hadn't killed them then Haarmann would finish them off by strangulation. Haarmann would keep any possessions his victims had and sell them on the black market. This wasn't the only thing he sold on the black market. He also sold meat. Could this meat have been the human flesh of his victims? That doesn't seem unlikely at all. Fritz Haarmann was no rocket scientist when it came to brains though. He wasn't exactly the most adept serial killer when it came to covering the tracks of his grisly deeds.

Haarmann had been dumping his victims in the Leine River (a river in Thuringia and Lower Saxony). Some of the bodies washed ashore - which led the police to investigate the river thoroughly. They dragged the river and found hundreds of human bones. From what they found the police estimated that there were over twenty victims at least in this river. Haarmann, because of his criminal history, ended up on a list of suspects and was placed under secret observation by the police. They saw him trying to pick up boys at the train station and decided to search his home. Haarmann's home was full of blood stains and he was swiftly arrested.

The trial of Fritz Haarmann, by now a notorious true crime celebrity, took place in 1924. It didn't last very long. He was found guilty of 24 murders and sentenced to death by beheading. Haarmann's lover Hans Grans was also sentenced to death. Grans knew of the murders and had even ended up with the possessions of some of the victims as gifts. The trial had a huge number of witnesses called to give evidence. Some of the neighbours of Haarmann testified that they had seen him carrying large sacks to the river at strange hours. Haarmann made a very full confession to the police anyway. He gave detailed and gruesome details on how he had used an axe and knives to dismember his victims after death. On April the 15th 1925, Fritz Haarmann was beheaded by Guillotine in the grounds of Hanover Prison. His last words were - "I repent, but I do not fear death."

SARAH HARDING

Sarah Harding was born in Ascot in 1981. Her real name was Sarah

Hardman but she changed it in protest after her father had an affair and left the family. She attended Stockport college and had all manner of jobs. She worked in a nightclub, Pizza Hut, and was even a debt collector at one point. Sarah was desperate to be famous and sang in pubs and social clubs. Because she was blonde and attractive she even sent her photographs to FHM magazine. Any teenager who wants to be famous these days has an obvious port of call in the form of the cheesy singing and talent competition shows so beloved of modern television companies. In 2002, Sarah Harding auditioned for the show Popstars: the Rivals and ended up being selected to form a new girl group named Girls Aloud. The other members were Cheryl Tweedy, Nadine Coyle, Nicola Roberts and Kimberley Walsh.

Even if they win a public vote in a talent show competition, there is no guarantee that a manufactured band will be successful or have any staying power and lasting appeal. Some of these talent show bands and singers sank without trace in the real world. That certainly wasn't the case with Girls Aloud though. Their first single Sound of the Underground went to number one in Britain and they never looked back. Girls Aloud were an instant success. Girl bands were a staple of British pop not that long ago but seem thin on the ground these days. The Spice Girls were followed by Girls Aloud, Sugarbabes, and All Saints. This was the heyday of the girl group.

Girls Aloud achieved twenty consecutive top ten singles (including four number ones) in Britain. They were the biggest selling girl group in Britain in their day and made millions. Though no girl group ever quite managed to replicate the Spice Girls phenomenon it was Girls Aloud who came the closest. What helped Girls Aloud was the fact that, considering they were a talent show band cobbled together by committee (though there is a rich tradition in this - look at The Monkees), their music was pretty good as far as disposable pop music goes and they were fun and likeable. Other girl groups like All Saints sometimes seemed to be taking themselves a bit too seriously but Girls Aloud were colourful and poppy and natural performers.

You'd probably say that Cheryl Tweedy (later Cheryl Cole) was sort of the 'breakout' star for a time and the most charismatic performer of Girls Aloud but they all played their part. Sarah Harding and

Cheryl Cole were the two members who ended up in the tabloids the most. They were the two biggest 'characters' in the band who the media tended to gravitate towards. In 2006 Sarah Harding signed a deal to model Ultimo lingerie. She was by now a very rich young woman and beginning to expand her interests.

Girls Aloud went on a hiatus in 2009 and then got back together in 2012. A year later though they finally split up. There tends to be a limited shelf life for bands of this type (a consequence of young fans getting older and moving onto something else) so Girls Aloud had a good run all things considered and there was always the prospect of an inevitable reunion tour somewhere down the line. The split of Girls Aloud wasn't the end of the world as far as Sarah Harding was concerned because her ambition had always been to move into acting. Sadly though, this detour into acting didn't prove as successful as she might have hoped.

Sarah had a small part in an atrocious British crime thriller called Bad Day and an equally small part in a (much better) BBC drama called Freefall. Sarah was then cast as Roxy in the comedy sequel St Trinian's 2: The Legend of Fritton's Gold (Sarah had a cameo in the first picture) but this film got terrible reviews and was quickly forgotten. If you think that was bad, well, Sarah was also in the Danny Dyer film Run For Your Wife. This was a comic farce with a cast that included Denise van Outen, Lionel Blair, and Christopher Biggins and every bit as bad as it sounds. Run For Your Wife is regarded to be one of the worst films ever made (0% on Rotten Tomatoes in case you were wondering) and not the sort of thing that is likely to be much of a launch pad for a career as a thespian. That was more or less the end of Sarah's acting career although she did appear in the soap opera Coronation Street some years later.

Sarah Harding took something of a dive into reality television at this point. Reality shows were by now abounding in ludicrous fashion but celebrities were never in short supply to appear on them because it was good money for a couple of weeks work. Sarah appeared on Tumble - a BBC show where contestants take part in gymnastics. Sarah also appeared on The Jump - a Channel 4 show where contestants take part in winter sports. She was also on Celebrity Masterchef and won Celebrity Big Brother 20 in 2017. The line-up of Celebrity Big Brother that year, save for the fake 'spiritual medium' and Most Haunted star (the late) Derek Acorah and a few others, was for the most part a sorry collection of obscure reality stars and YouTubers. Sarah Harding was by some considerable distance the most famous person in the house.

Sarah also continued to dabble in music - although a planned solo album failed to appear. Sarah had several relationships but she was never married. One of her great ambitions was to have children. Fate though was about to deal Sarah a cruel and unexpected blow. In August 2020, during the lockdowns, Sarah Harding was diagnosed with breast cancer. She wrote - "At first I thought it was just a cyst. I'd been playing my guitar a lot, and I thought the strap had probably irritated an area around my breast. The trouble was, the pain was getting worse. It got so bad that I couldn't sleep in a bed any more. I slept on the sofa, popping painkillers like they were Smarties. One day I woke up realising that I'd been in denial."

Sarah began chemotherapy and used CBD oil to ease her pain. She enjoyed Christmas because she knew it might be her last. The cancer had spread to other parts of her body so it was not a good prognosis. It was somewhat surreal for everyone to learn that Sarah Harding was very ill because not only was she still quite young and still very famous, she had always seemed such a vibrant and healthy person. Sarah continued to write songs during this difficult time and also completed a memoir - which spoke a lot about her cancer battle. She refused to have radiotherapy because she couldn't bear the thought of losing her trademark blonde hair.

Although there were hopes that Sarah might beat her cancer and make a full recovery (in the fashion that Kylie Minogue did when she had breast cancer), sadly it wasn't to be.

Sarah Harding died in Manchester on the morning of 5 September 2021, at the age of 39. Her mother wrote - "It is with deep heartbreak that today I'm sharing the news that my beautiful daughter Sarah has sadly passed away. I know she won't want to be remembered for her fight against this terrible disease - she was a bright shining star and I hope that's how she can be remembered instead."

Tributes flooded in from the world of music and entertainment when Sarah died. Sarah's fellow Girl Aloud members were of course devastated. The funeral and burial details of Sarah Harding were kept secret by the family and not revealed to the public. When she was alive, Sarah said though that she had left instructions on what she wanted. Most of all she wanted something funny on her headstone. It was a great shock to those who grew up with Girls Aloud to think that one of the band members was no longer with us because they always radiated boundless youth, energy, and - most of all - fun. Sarah Harding will always live on though in all the pop videos and songs.

EVEL KNIEVEL

The daredevil motorcycle stunt rider Evel Knievel became something of a superhero to American children in the seventies with his alarmingly dangerous exploits on ABC's Wide World of Sports. Knievel was sort of like Elvis on a motorbike and shared the King's fondness for capes and white jumpsuits as he attempted all manner of bonkers stunts involving buses, canyons and even a rocket. His stunts frequently went wrong though and he is apparently in the Guiness Book of Records for breaking more bones in one year than any other person. He even spent 29 days in a coma after his attempt to jump the water fountains outside Caesars Palace in Las Vegas went completely wrong. At the height of his fame he travelled around the world with a huge entourage and was paid millions.

However, despite his popularity and young fanbase, Knievel wasn't a particularly nice person. He started life as a petty criminal and gambled away his fortune when he was a celebrity. He was a hard-drinking womaniser and tarnished his reputation forever when he brutally attacked a former promoter (who had criticised him in a book) with a baseball bat. He was part of a triumvirate of great American entertainers in that decade. There was Elvis, Muhammad Ali and Evel Knievel. They were all living legends in their own way and shared a sense of the flamboyant and a love of theatrics. Knievel - born Robert Craig Knievel in 1938 - was certainly the least loveable of the three though.

Robert Craig Knievel began life as a small time criminal who was an expert at cracking safes. Knievel used to scarper from police on his motorbike and when he saw a stunt rider jumping over cars at a small fair he hit upon the idea of doing this himself. He decided he would become the greatest and most daring stunt rider of all.

Knievel was clever in the way he realised you had to have an angle to draw attention to yourself and also try to do things that no one had done. In one of his earliest stunts he jumped over a box containing 100 rattlesnakes! Some of the stunts Knievel attempted were absolutely bizarre. In 1974 he strapped himself into an experimental rocket in an attempt to cross a 2,000-foot wide canyon at 'Snake River'. The rocket was launched from a ramp and had to reach over 300 mph to get him over the canyon. It all went wrong but - just for once - Knievel made a safe landing with the aid of a parachute.

Why did he attempt such nutty things? Well, the money was obviously an incentive (he was paid $6 million for the Snake River stunt) but he was genuinely fearless. He said he loved the thrill of flying through the air and staring down death and, just generally, being Evel Knievel and the macho world of groupies and fast living. "You can't ask a guy like me why I performed. I really wanted to fly through the air. I was a daredevil, a performer. I loved the thrill, the money, the whole macho thing. All those things made me Evel Knievel. Sure, I was scared. You gotta be an ass not to be scared. But I beat the hell out of death. [...] You're in the air for four seconds, you're part of the machine, and then if you make a mistake midair, you say to yourself, "Oh, boy. I'm gonna crash," and there's nothing you can do to stop it, not at all."

When Knievel had a terrible crash - like attempting to leap over Double-Decker buses in London - he would usually end up doing the stunt again in the future and often succeed where he had failed before. He was best remembered for his crashes though and an unavoidable element of the popularity of his stunts was that the watching audience never knew what was going to happen. An entire generation of children watched Knievel's stunts on television through their fingers, the tension so great they could barely stand it.

Knievel had a circus like entourage that traveled around in a convoy like a pop group in the seventies and once said that he made $60 million and blew $63 million. Not unsurprisingly, Knievel's health collapsed later in life and his battered body was beset with problems. Then there was Knievel's baseball bat assault on Shelly Saltman, who had worked on the Snake River promotion and wrote (according to Knievel) unflattering things about the stunt rider. Knievel got six months in jail and Saltman was awarded $13 million in damages (not that he ever got any of this money).

The attack on the promoter came three months after the release of Viva Knievel!, a famously terrible 1977 film where Knievel played himself. The revelation that Knievel was apparently a violent thug in real life damaged the box-office and it was barely released abroad. Knievel also lost his lucrative sponsorship and marketing deals. Knievel was now broke. His money was gone and his health collapsed. He died in 2007 at the age of 69 - though not before he had been slightly rehabilitated somewhat in the public eye with some awards and recognition. It's a miracle really that he lived that long. In the end he could barely breathe or walk. The seventies superstar became a faded cult memory to people who were children in that decade. They would never quite forget though that crazy charismatic man flying through the air on his bike.

TRENT LEHMAN

Trent Lehman, born in Los Angeles in 1961, was a child actor famous for his part in comedy show Nanny & the Professor with Juliet Mills and Richard Long. This show ran for 53 episodes at the start of the 1970s. Lehman played the middle kid 'Butch' in the show. Nanny & the Professor sort of cashed in on the popularity of Marry Poppins and had Mills as a mysterious and possibly magical British nanny who arrives unexpectedly in an American family home. Juliet Mills is the sister of former Disney star Hayley Mills. Their father was the famous actor Sir John Mills. John Mills actually made a few cameos in Nanny & the Professor - which was nice.

The other kids in Nanny & the Professor were played by David

Doremus and Kim Richards. Doremus later had a reccuring role in The Waltons and then became manager of an electronics company. As for Kim Richards, she was in literally everything after Nanny & the Professor ended. She was the little girl who gets shot after buying an ice cream in John Carpenter's Assault on Precinct 13. She was also in Little House on the Prairie, The Dukes of Hazzard, Magnum P.I., Meatballs II, Escape to Witch Mountain. In recent years she has been a regular on The Real Housewives of Beverly Hills and her nieces include Nicky and Paris Hilton. She was even in a Sharknado film for heaven's sake.

David Doremus and Kim Richards did just fine thank you very much after Nanny & the Professor ended but that wasn't the case for poor Trent Lehman. Trent was destined, like Bobby Driscoll, to be one of those Hollywood kids who is completely forgotten. Prior to Nanny & the Professor, Trent Lehman had appeared in Gunsmoke and a film called The Christine Jorgensen Story. After the end of Nanny & the Professor, Lehman, like so many child stars, found it tough to get any work at all. He appeared in the medical show Emergency! and did a little bit of voice acting but his last credit was in 1973. Hollywood was more or less finished with Lehman after this and he ended up living in Colorado with his mother - his days as a child star now a distant memory.

It must be very strange indeed to be famous as a kid but then have this fame suddenly stripped away. Trent basically had to learn how to be a normal person again. His early life had revolved around acting and television studios. That was all gone now. When he got a bit older, Lehman decided to move back to Los Angeles to be closer to his girlfriend. Maybe a part of him still fostered hopes that he could somehow get back into acting. Moving back to Los Angeles though turned out to be one of the worst decisions Trent Lehman ever made. When his girlfriend split up with him, Trent - by all accounts - did not take this rejection very well at all.

It was later said by their friends that Trent and his girlfriend had lost most of their money and possessions in Los Angeles when they were victims of a burglary. This had caused a great strain in their relationship. Oddly though, Lehman and his girlfriend had not reported this incident to the police. The speculation is that Trent's use of narcotics is why he didn't want the police nosing around his life and home. The robbery added more gloom to Trent's already troubled state of mind.

Trent was somewhat aimless in his life now and drinking a bit too much. He ended staying with an old school friend in Los Angeles but it must have been apparent to his friend that Trent was a bit of a lost soul and struggling to find his new place in the world. On January 17, 1982, Trent was with some friends and alarmed one of them when he asked for a gun. He said he wanted to shoot himself. They maybe shrugged this off as a flippant statement by someone who was becoming sozzled.

Early in the evening the friends dropped off Trent, who was quite drunk by now, near his van. They advised him to get some sleep because he was due in court the next day because of a traffic offense. The van was parked near Vena Avenue Elementary School in Pacoima. Trent had actually attended this school himself when he was younger and starring in Nanny & the Professor. The school must have reminded Trent of happier more innocent days in the city. Around two in the morning, Trent's friends decided to go back and check on him. They expected to find him asleep in the van sleeping off the booze but he wasn't there. They were worried when they saw that their friend had left the van. Where had he gone at this hour?

The van was littered with empty beer bottles - which obviously indicated that the already sozzled Trent had carried on drinking alone in the vehicle. Lehman's friends then had a look around the immediate area and made a horrifying and tragic discovery. Trent had hanged himself on a chain link fence outside the school. He had made a noose from a bandana. Trent had used a green bucket to stand on and kick away. Before he killed himself, Trent had even written an impromptu will on his court document and put it in his back pocket. He didn't have much in the world but the note said he wanted his mother to have everything. Although he hadn't been hanging there for very long, Trent was already dead. He was just 20 years old.

An autopsy established that there was cocaine in Trent Lehman's system in addition to the copious amounts of alcohol he had drunk.

Trent was cremated in Los Angeles and his ashes were given to his mother. Trent was described as unemployed at the time of his death. It seems that he struggled to work out what to do with his life once his acting career came to an end. Trent's stepfather said that Trent planned to become a carpenter. Trent just wanted an ordinary stable happy life but he never managed to get clear headed enough to make this happen. There wasn't an awful lot of press about Trent's death. Those who had fond memories of Nanny & the Professor would always remember him though as the mop-topped Bentley "Butch" Everett.

Trent's tragic death was one of the motivations for the founding of A Minor Consideration. A Minor Consideration is a non-profit foundation created to provide guidance and support for young child performers, past, present and future. It focuses on the welfare and treatment of child actors both during their employment in the film and television industry but also (and here's the really crucial bit) following the END of their careers. This was the sort of organisation that Trent Lehman could have done with when his own short career in Hollywood fizzled out. Sadly, it seems that Trent Lehman was rather forgotten in Hollywood and never got the help and guidance he desperately needed.

STEPHEN MILLIGAN

Stephen Milligan was born in Surrey in 1948. He studied at Oxford and then became a journalist. He worked for The Economist, The Sunday Times and the BBC amongst others. Milligan decided to go into politics after journalism and at the 1992 general election was elected as the Conservative Member of Parliament for Eastleigh. Milligan was on the moderate wing of the party - which tallied fairly well with John Major (who was obviously the Prime Minister and Conservative leader at the time). As such, Milligan was seen as something of a rising star and someone who would potentially hold one of the big offices of state somewhere down the line.

Milligan's particular field of expertise - or interest if you prefer - in the House of Commons seemed to be foreign affairs. This was clearly a consequence of his time as a journalist reporting on stories from abroad. Milligan was very popular in politics and journalism and had a lot of friends. People who knew him said that he was funny and clever. Milligan could seem a bit socially inept and ill at ease though when he had to go to functions or meet the public. He seemed like a happy enough person though who was enjoying his new life in the world of politics. He was quite well thought of by his constituents because he spent most of his time in Hampshire and didn't forget who he was supposed to be representing. What happened next to Stephen Milligan though was truly beyond belief.

On the 7th of February 1994, Milligan's secretary Vera Taggart went to his home in Chiswick to see him because Milligan had not turned up at the House of Commons that morning. This was most unlike Stephen Milligan. There was no answer at the door so Vera Taggert used a hidden key to let herself in. Taggert was met with a shocking discovery in the kitchen. The 45 year-old Milligan was dead at the table. He had an electrical flex wrapped around his neck, a slice of orange in his mouth, a bin liner over his head, and he was wearing nothing except a pair of ladies stockings. Vera Taggart was doubtless shocked and shaken by this awful sight. She quickly telephoned the emergency services and waited for them to arrive. It was later estimated that Milligan had been dead for about 48 hours when he was found.

The police made something of a blunder when they arrived because there was some sort of leak and a number of Milligan's relatives heard about his - on the face of it rather odd and tawdry - death on the radio before they had been informed by the authorities. As you might imagine the relatives were very angry about this lack of protocol and simple plain decency. The inquest ruled that Milligan had died as a result of 'misadventure'. For 'misadventure' read auto-erotic asphyxiation. This is the (highly bizarre and dangerous) act of starving oneself of oxygen to heighten sexual pleasure. Amyl nitrite, GHB, or nitrous oxide are often used by those who participate in this act. The segment of orange in the mouth in auto-erotic asphyxiation is to quash the bitter taste of the amyl nitrate.

Auto-erotic asphyxiation has been around for centuries - though fatalities remain rare. One of the most famous auto-erotic asphyxiation deaths was that of Reverend Gary Aldridge, who served as the pastor for Montgomery's Thorington Road Baptist Church. In 2007, Aldridge was found dead in his home due to auto-erotic asphyxiation. He was wearing two rubber diving suits and had a dildo in his bottom. The District Attorney for Montgomery County and Aldridge's church did their best to keep the autopsy findings secret but the truth leaked out in the end. You can't really blame them for trying to brush that one under the carpet.

Milligan's death was embarrassing for John Major because he'd just launched something which he called 'back to basics' - which was a crusade against sleaze and corruption or something. It was all pretty meaningless waffle as a number of Major's MP's continued to have extra-marital affairs and take back-handers. Major even had an affair himself while he was Prime Minister. In the aftermath of Stephen Milligan's death, John Major remarked that Milligan must have been desperately unhappy. Major seemed to mistakenly have presumed that Milligan committed suicide - which was clearly not the case. If you are going to intentionally commit suicide you are hardly likely to do so in ladies stockings with a bin liner over your head!

One of Stephen Milligan's cousins took issue with Major's comment and wrote a letter to the newspaper in which he said - "Stephen was neither miserable or unhappy. On the contrary, he was thoroughly fulfilled and happy in his work in Westminster and his Eastleigh constituency, which gave him the chance to be of service to others as he always wished." Milligan's friends and relatives were very unhappy at the way the death was being reported - as if Stephen was some sort of crazed lonely sexual deviant.

Stephen Milligan was buried in St Peter's Churchyard in West Sussex. Life went on in Westminster and Milligan became a sort of weird punchline - the MP who died with a bag over his head. The makers of the satirical television programme Have I Got News For You even sent out oranges, stockings, and bin liners to promote a new season. The BBC had to offer an apology for this stupid bad taste stunt - and rightly so. Stephen Milligan had become a macabre joke due to the strange nature of his death.

Milligan's relatives, former girlfriends, and his friends from the world of journalism had serious doubts about the way his death had been presented in the media and inquests. . There was something about his death which didn't feel right to them. They suspected foul play. Was it at all possible that Stephen Milligan was murdered and it was then made to look like an erotic asphyxiation accident? The esteemed BBC journalist John Simpson was a friend of Stephen Milligan. Simpson found it hard to believe that his friend, who went to church and was alarmingly normal, could really have died in such bizarre fashion.

Simpson noted that, in his career as a journalist, Stephen Milligan had uncovered various dodgy stuff going on in Russia and had even talked about writing a book on the subject one day. Simpson said that - suspiciously - critics of the Yeltsin government had sometimes been found dead in circumstances which suggested auto-erotic asphyxiation. The clear theory in Simpson's mind then is that Milligan might have been murdered by the KGB. That might sound like something out of a spy novel but we know only too well these days that the Russians are capable of these sorts of acts. The Russian angle is one theory but there is another too which is somewhat closer to home.

Another theory is that Milligan was one of several journalists killed by the British secret services because they threatened to blow the whistle on government involvement in illegal arms sales. Gerald James, a businessman who was caught up in the 'arms to Iraq' scandal, wrote a memoir in which he said that an MI6 spy turned journalist was found dead in circumstances very similar to Milligan. There was another connection too because just before he died the man in question apparently talked of suspecting foul play in Milligan's death. Stephen Milligan was the Parliamentary Private Secretary to Jonathan Aitken - who was the defence procurement minister. Stephen Milligan would therefore have had knowledge of sensitive British government documents when it came to defence and weapons sales.

Another suspicious detail in this case is that MI5 allegedly cleared out Milligan's office of documents after his death and police officers were seen carrying bags out Milligan's home after his body was discovered. Perhaps the most interesting evidence suggesting a conspiracy is that Milligan was found in his kitchen. This was an area where neighbours could see into his house and where anyone could walk in. If you were going to engage in auto-erotic asphyxiation would you really pick this room? Wouldn't you go somewhere more private like a bedroom?

The kitchen ties into the murder theory because it meant Milligan's (with bin liner and all) body was easy to find. Another curious detail is that no drugs were found in Milligan's system or in the house - which is atypical for an auto-erotic asphyxiation death. If there was no amyl nitrate why did Milligan have a piece of orange in his mouth? That doesn't make any sense. Was Stephen Milligan murdered or was this a simple case of a sex game gone wrong (misadventure as the coroner might say)? We simply don't know for sure. The jury, for now, is still out.

MYA-LECIA NAYLOR

Mya-Lecia Naylor was born in Warwickshire in 2002. She was educated at Royal Russell School and Coloma Convent Girls' School. It was certainly an early start in showbusiness for Mya-Lecia because she appeared in the sitcom Absolutely Fabulous while still a toddler. Mya-Lecia also sang from a young age and had ambitions to launch a music career one day in conjunction with her acting. She also did a number of commercials. In 2011, Mya-Lecia was the lead in a short lived kids show called Tati's Hotel. The show was about a magical hotel. In 2013, Mya-Lecia had a brush with Hollywood when she appeared in the big budget film Cloud Atlas. She also had a small part in a zombie film called Code Red.

Mya-Lecia Naylor would become best known though for her role as Fran in the BBC children's channel sitcom Millie Inbetween. She played this role from 2014 to 2018. Millie Inbetween, which revolved around its young lead Millie Innes, was a likeable enough kids sitcom about family life and Mya-Lecia Naylor's role in the show steadily grew as she got older. Many big stars began their careers in kids shows and Mya-Lecia seemed to be following this well trodden path. A show like Millie Inbetween was good training for any child actor.

Mya-Lecia's next role was in another BBC kids show - Almost
Never. Almost Never was a sort of musical comedy about two
fictitious bands which formed out of talent show success. Mya-Lecia
played Mya, a member of the band Girls Here (who were apparently
based on Little Mix). Almost Never was popular enough to
eventually be picked up by the Disney Channel but - alas - Mya-
Lecia would not live to see this. Away from the screen Mya-Lecia
was building up her YouTube channel - where she shared beauty and
lifestyle tips and generally goofed around in amusing teenage
fashion. The YouTube channel was like a sort of diary of her day
and the things she got up to.

Mya-Lecia came across as unpretentious and likeable in her
YouTube videos. She didn't seem like someone who took themselves
too seriously or had got too big for their boots through
showbusiness. As of yet though Mya-Lecia was only a familiar face
to the young people who watched CBBC. She hoped to branch out as
she got older and do many different things. Before she died there
was actually a lot of speculation that Mya-Lecia Naylor had been
cast in the (then forthcoming) Netflix show The Witcher.

Mya-Lecia was a mixed-race teenager with curly haired good looks
and those that worked with her all said she was funny and popular.
Mya-Lecia Naylor seemed to have a bright future ahead in whatever
she chose to do. Stardom certainly seemed attainable for this bright
and photogenic kid. Sadly though she was destined to join the sad
ranks of child stars who met a tragically premature end. On 7 April
2019, Mya-Lecia was found hanging in her home in South London
by her mother early in the morning. She was rushed to Croydon
University Hospital but had gone into cardiac arrest and was
pronounced dead about 90 minutes after she was found. Mya-Lecia
Naylor was just sixteen years-old.

There were no drugs or alcohol in Mya-Lecia's system and after an
investigation and inquest her death was ruled as one of
'misadventure'. What this essentially means is that someone did
something dangerous but did NOT actually mean to harm
themselves. It is certainly not believed that Mya-Lecia intended to

kill herself. That simply made this tragedy all the more tragic and heartbreaking. Her father said she had been grounded and banned from going to a party and he believes this is why she staged this 'stunt'. "I honestly believe she was just making some sort of point," he told the coroner's court.

Mya-Lecia was also said to be 'stressed' about her impending school exams - but not to the extent that she was suicidal. Most teenagers get stressed about exams. It is perfectly normal. Mya-Lecia's phones and laptop were checked by the police for signs of anything suspicious but there was nothing at all on them to indicate she was thinking of taking her life. In fact, in her last ever interview she had talked about how excited she was for the future and alluded to some upcoming project she wasn't allowed to talk about (the mysterious upcoming project was more than likely The Witcher). Mya-Lecia had spent her last night happily watching a film with her family. They hadn't noticed anything ominous about her behaviour or mood.

All in all, it was an unbearably sad and tragic waste of a life that had barely begun. Mya-Lecia Naylor was someone who seemed destined to become very famous indeed one day. Those that had grown up watching Millie Inbetween were shocked when they heard the news. It hardly seemed believable that the cute kid they'd watched grow-up on the small screen was no longer with us. It was especially surreal and sad for those who had worked with Mya-Lecia on her BBC shows.

"Devastated for Mya," said Millie Innes, Mya-Lecia's co-star on Millie Inbetween. "The pain of her passing has been awful. Mya and I grew up together over the past five years and had an extremely close relationship. I will always cherish our friendship and the moments we spent together beautiful girl. I am devastated and heartbroken." Elaine Sperber, who was the Executive Producer of Millie Inbetween, said - "She was a joy to work with on the whole series. She really grew into the role of Fran and made it uniquely her own. An enormously talented and totally lovely girl, she was also great fun to have around, and was much loved by the whole cast and crew."

The BBC issued a statement in which they said - "We are so sorry to have to tell you that Mya-Lecia, who you will know from 'Millie Inbetween' and 'Almost Never' has, very sadly, died. Mya-Lecia was a much loved part of the BBC Children's family, and a hugely talented actress, singer and dancer. We will miss her enormously and we are sure that you will want to join us in sending all our love to her family and friends." The director of CBBC said it was 'unthinkable' that the channel would now face the future without Mya-Lecia because she had always been such a cherished part of the network.

Mya-Lecia died three months after the debut of the first episode of Almost Never. Out of respect it was decided not to recast Mya-Lecia's character Mya. What they did in the second season of Almost Never was say that Mya had left the girl group in the show after their less than successful European tour. Mya-Lecia's death meant the second season of Almost Never had to be re-written because she was due to play a much larger role than she had in the first season. The screenwriter Simon Underwood said that at the time of Mya-Lecia's death he had been writing a children's drama specifically with her in mind as the lead.

Mya-Lecia Naylor's memorial took place at the Our Lady of the Annunciation Churchyard, Croydon. It's a cliche to say that someone was taken too soon but in Mya-Lecia's case that was sadly all too true. We'll never know what she would have gone on to do or how famous she might have become. It's seems safe to say though that her fame and career would eventually have gone far beyond the realm of CBBC.

RICHARD RAMIREZ

Richard Ramirez was born in El Paso, Texas, in 1960. Ramirez was a terrifying killer known as The Night Stalker. Ramirez suffered two head injuries as a child. It is believed they left him with seizures. His childhood was not exactly helped by his adoration of a cousin who served in Vietnam. This cousin filled the head of Ramirez with tales (and often photographic evidence) of war atrocities and also taught Ramirez how to use a knife. The cousin of Ramirez later shot his own wife while Ramirez was present. Richard Ramirez was pretty messed up from a young age. He would sometimes sleep in a graveyard to get away from his violent father. He was also obsessed with Satanism and took a lot of drugs. Pretty soon he was thief and rapist. The Ramirez story would get a lot worse though.

Ramirez got a job in a Holiday Inn as a young man. As you might imagine, he didn't last very long. He stole from the customers and tried to rape one of the guests. In 1984, Ramirez raped and murdered 9-year-old Mei Leung and hung her body from a drainpipe. This was his first murder (although it was only decades later through DNA evidence that this was established) and his killing spree began. Ramirez would stage home invasions in the Los Angeles and San Francisco area. He would usually shoot any men men he found in a house and then rape and kill the women. Ramirez would sometime daub occult symbols in the houses where he had killed. He left the eyes of one victim in a jewel box for the authorities to find. Ramirez nearly decapitated one victim by slashing her in the throat multiple times.

Ramirez was a very evil and disturbed man. He once attacked two sisters in their eighties - one of whom was disabled. He raped the women and used a cord to give one of them an electric shock. One of the sisters died and the other survived. Ramirez would use anything to hand to kill people. Some victims were killed with a machete or tire iron. His gruesome and harrowing activities (which left dozens of people terribly injured in addition to those that died) of Richard Ramirez lasted for a year. The police had matched a fingerprint from a stolen car to Ramirez (who was obviously known to the police for previous crimes) and deduced that Ramirez matched the description of The Night Stalker given by a victim who had survived. The young man who supplied the information that helped capture Ramirez was highly reluctant to claim the reward because he didn't want people on the street to think he was a police informant.

Richard Ramirez was captured after his picture was circulated by the authorities. Ramirez was in a Los Angeles store and held down by members of the public until the police arrived. The trial of Richard Ramirez was the most expensive Los Angeles had ever seen at the time thanks to its slow pace and jury troubles. During the preparation for the Richard Ramirez trial, one of the jurors was shot dead. This created much publicity with speculation that Ramirez had somehow orchestrated the death from prison to influence the jury. There was of course no actual truth to this rumour. He wasn't some criminal mastermind or occult magician. He was just a sick and evil man sitting in a prison cell.

Ramirez wore sunglasses during his trial and acted as if he was a celebrity. On September 20, 1989, Ramirez was convicted of 13 counts of murder, 5 attempted murders, 11 sexual assaults, and 14 burglaries. He was sentenced to death. Richard Ramirez surprised people when he appeared on television in a prison interview because he seemed completely sane and calm and shrewdly didn't take the bait whenever the interviewer tried to rile him or make him confess. When the actor Sean Penn (who was famously obstreperous and known to punch journalists) served some time in L.A County jail in 1987, he discovered that Richard Ramirez was in the same prison. Ramirez had a fan letter passed to Penn.

Richard Ramirez was said to get plenty of fan mail in prison from women when he was arrested. When he was in prison, Ramirez married magazine editor Doreen Lioy. Lioy had been sending him dozens of letters. Doreen Lioy described Ramirez (who, lest we forget, once plucked out a victim's eyes and put them in a jewelry case for the police to find) as funny and charming. If that's not hybristophilia then nothing is. "I think he's a really great person. He's my best friend; he's my buddy," said Lioy. "I can't help the way the world looks at him. They don't know him the way I do. [People call me crazy] or stupid or lying, and I'm none of those things. I just believe in him completely. In my opinion, there was far more evidence to convict O.J. Simpson, and we all know how that turned out."

Ramirez was never executed in the end. He died of secondary to B-cell lymphoma in 2013 at the age of 53. Doreen Lioy didn't seem to turn up to claim the body of Ramirez when he died in prison. Maybe she was in love with some other evil incarcerated serial killer by this time. In 2009 it had been proven beyond doubt by DNA technology that Richard Ramirez killed a nine year old girl named Mei Leung in 1984. Even the deluded and gullible Doreen Lioy must have felt very stupid and very appalled and disgusted by this scientific cold case revelation. Lioy was not the only person to find Ramirez attractive. Cynthia Haden, one of the jurors at his trial, fell in love with Ramirez and defended him in interviews.

Ramirez was a truly terrifying and crazy man. "You don't understand me," he said. "You are not expected to. You are not capable. I am beyond your experience. I am beyond good and evil. I will be avenged. Lucifer dwells in all of us...I don't believe in the hypocritical, moralistic dogma of this so-called civilized society....You maggots make me sick! Hypocrites one and all...I don't need to hear all of society's rationalizations. I've heard them all before...legions of the night, night breed, repeat not the errors of the night prowler and show no mercy." These days, a signed self-portrait by Richard Ramirez (from when he was in prison obviously) can sell for around $3,500. Strange but true - Ramirez was a big fan of the Marvel Comics character Iron Man and used to draw Iron Man sketches in prison.

JONBENET RAMSEY

JonBenét Ramsey was born on August 6, 1990, in Atlanta, Georgia. JonBenét was the daughter of businessman John Bennett Ramsey and Patsy Ramsey. Patsy competed in beauty pageants herself when she was younger and had moulded JonBenét into a child beauty pageant queen. Child beauty pageants are considered rather odd and even distasteful by many. They often involve dressing up little kids as if they are adults. JonBenét also had a nine year-old brother named Burke. In the early hours of December 26, 1996, the Ramseys noticed that their daughter seemed to be missing. They then claimed that they found a ransom note at the bottom of the stairs left by an apparent kidnapper.

The ransom note read as follows - 'Mr. Ramsey, Listen carefully! We are a group of individuals that represent a small foreign faction. We do respect your bussiness [sic] but not the country that it serves. At this time we have your daughter in our posession [sic]. She is safe and unharmed and if you want her to see 1997, you must follow our instructions to the letter. You will withdraw $118,000.00 from your account. $100,000 will be in $100 bills and the remaining $18,000 in $20 bills. Make sure that you bring an adequate size attache to the bank. When you get home you will put the money in a brown paper bag. I will call you between 8 and 10 am tomorrow to instruct you on delivery. The delivery will be exhausting so I advise you to be rested. If we monitor you getting the money early, we might call you early to arrange an earlier delivery of the money and hence a [sic] earlier delivery pick-up of your daughter.

'Any deviation of my instructions will result in the immediate execution of your daughter. You will also be denied her remains for proper burial. The two gentlemen watching over your daughter do not particularly like you so I advise you not to provoke them. Speaking to anyone about your situation, such as Police, F.B.I., etc., will result in your daughter being beheaded. If we catch you talking to a stray dog, she dies. If you alert bank authorities, she dies. If the money is in any way marked or tampered with, she dies.

'You will be scanned for electronic devices and if any are found, she dies. You can try to deceive us but be warned that we are familiar with law enforcement countermeasures and tactics. You stand a 99% chance of killing your daughter if you try to out smart [sic] us. Follow our instructions and you stand a 100% chance of getting her back. You and your family are under constant scrutiny as well as the authorities. Don't try to grow a brain John. You are not the only fat cat around so don't think that killing will be difficult. Don't underestimate us John. Use that good southern common sense of yours. It is up to you now John! Victory!'

Despite the clear instructions in the ransom note not to involve the police, the Ramseys immediately called them. The police arrived at the house around 6am but their handling of the immediate crime scene left something to be desired. Friends and family were allowed to wander around (potentially destroying forensic evidence) and the parents were not formally interviewed individually straight away. In cases this like this the first thing the police are supposed to do is to investigate the family and relatives and friends of the family to make sure none of them were involved in the crime. That evidently wasn't done as soon as it could have been.

Linda Ardndt was the first police officer on the scene. She noted that there were no footprints in the snow which suggested an intruder. She also found John Bennett Ramsey suspicious (another detective said that he later heard John Bennett Ramsey make a secret phone call a few hours after the body was discovered in which he was attempting to book a flight to Atlanta). The police asked the parents to check to see if anything was amiss in the house. Incredibly, none of the police officers had yet to check the basement (which would appear to have been an obvious place to look). John Bennett Ramsey went down there himself - where he found the dead body of his daughter JonBenét. JonBenét Ramsey had been strangled and her skull was fractured. Her mouth was covered in duct tape and her wrists and neck were bound.

John Bennett Ramsey carried the dead body of his daughter upstairs - thus contaminating both the body and murder scene. There was no evidence of rape but JonBenét Ramsey HAD suffered some form of sexual assault. It was established that her private parts and upper legs had been wiped clean by the killer. It turned out that the ransom note had been written on stationary which belonged to the Ramseys. This alleged intruder had even used a pen from the house. This was a pretty odd detail. If you have just broken into a house and murdered a child would you really stick around in the house and calmly take the time to write a three page ransom note? Wouldn't you just get out of there as fast as you could?

And why was the killer writing a ransom note for a dead child left in the house? None of this made any sense. The ransom note was pretty bizarre with curious details like the mention of John Bennett Ramsey's business. Any why was a kidnapper telling the parents to be 'rested'? The ransom note was deemed highly suspicious by those who have studied this case. The handwriting of the family was studied by the police in relation to the ransom note but their findings were apparently inconclusive. There are some claims though in articles about this case that independent handwriting experts judged Patsy to have been the likely author of the strange ransom note.

There are basically two theories in this awful case. Theory number one is that someone in the Ramsey family killed JonBenét - whether by intent or accident - and they then tried to cover it up. Theory number two is that an intruder broke into the house while they were asleep and murdered JonBenét. Both of these theories, as we shall see, have evidence supporting them and evidence contradicting them. It's safe to say that the murder of JonBenét Ramsey is puzzling to say the least.

Regarding the theory that someone in the family killed JonBenét, well, there were certainly some crumbs for those inclined to lean towards this theory. Some of the police detectives noted that John Bennett Ramsey seemed strangely unemotional given the circumstances - which struck them as odd. It could be that he was simply in shock although detectives also noted that both parents seemed curiously disinterested in the ransom note and its stipulations. They soon seemed to completely forget about it.

If you really did find your child missing one morning and then discover a ransom note with instructions and deadlines, well, you might think that one would be a lot more inclined to worry about the details of the note than the Ramseys were that day. There are generally three floated armchair detective scenarios for the theory that the family were involved. The first scenario is that the father was sexually abusing JonBenét and killed her to ensure her silence. Maybe it was an accident and the mother helped cover it up. These are the sorts of theories which have flourished around this dreadful case.

The parents probably didn't help their case at the time either by refusing to take a police lie detector test. This was presumably done of the advice of their legal advisors. The second scenario is that the mother Patsy killed JonBenét. The main problem with this theory is motive. Why on earth would a mother kill her six year-old daughter? A common theory is that Patsy snapped because JonBenét kept wetting the bed. The family housekeeper believed that Patsy had killed JonBenét and went public about this. It's safe to say that a cloud of suspicion dogged the parents in the aftermath of this tragedy and never really went away. It should be noted though that no DNA evidence conclusively proved either parent was involved and they were never formally charged with anything.

A very popular theory in this case is that JonBenét's brother Burke killed her by accident or intentionally and then the parents made it look like an 'intruder murder' to protect their son. A baseball bat belonging to Burke was found in the house but Burke's father had told the police Burke didn't have a baseball bat. Pineapple was found in JonBenét's stomach and Burke was eating a bowl of pineapple the night before. The reason why the pineapple comes up in theories about this case is that the night before her disappearance the parents said they took JonBenét from their car asleep and put her straight to bed.

The family had been out to eat but they did not eat any pineapple. It is therefore presumed by some that they were lying about JonBenét going straight to bed because she MUST have eaten some pineapple in the house - and if she was eating pineapple with Burke he must have been one of the last people to see her. If the parents lied about this what else were they lying about? It should be noted at this point that Burke has always vehemently denied any blame for his sister's death and taken legal action against those who suggest otherwise. Burke, by now a software engineer, did a television interview with Dr Phil in 2016. He smiled throughout the interview and came across as childlike and a trifle weird.

As for the intruder theory, the police did later establish that a handprint and unknown DNA was found in the house. Forensics indicated that two unknown people could have been in the house that night but - frustratingly - they've never been identified on any DNA database. In fact, later DNA advances led the police to officially state the parents were innocent and the intruder theory was most likely true. Not everyone is convinced by that though.

One weird detail is that neighbours said they heard screams coming from the Ramsey house that tragic night but the Ramsey parents claimed they didn't hear anything. That was definitely another odd and strange detail which made no sense. If there were screams as the neighbours claim then the Ramseys must surely have heard them as they were much closer what with them being in the ACTUAL house. It seems that the intruder, if this theory is correct, must have abducted JonBenét and taken her to the basement. Weirdly though the police didn't find much evidence of a break in and the ransom note (which was found by Patsy) remains rather puzzling and suspicious.

Forensic investigator Werner Spitz, in a CBS documentary, suggested that JonBenét was killed when she was struck with a flashlight. The documentary tended to lean towards the theory that Burke was responsible. However, no DNA from JonBenét or Burke was found on flashlights in the house according to the police. The autopsy found wounds on JonBenét's back which were believed to have come from a stun gun. Werner Spitz believed the wounds came from the toy train tracks belonging to Burke. If this was a game of Cluedo, Spitz had Burke in the basement by means of flashlight and toy train track. Burke Ramsey sued CBS and was awarded millions when he heard about this documentary.

John Bennett Ramsey and Patsy Ramsey were formally cleared as suspects by the police in 2008. Patsy did not live to see this though as she died of cancer in 2006. DNA from JonBenét also indicated that an unknown person had been there in the house that night. To this day people online still venture forth with theories that one of the parents killed JonBenét but - officially at least - they were cleared. There have been many suspects in this case but thus far they've had alibis or proved to be red herrings. The police have interviewed around 600 people but no one has been charged or convicted for JonBenét's death.

Outside of the Ramsey family, the other suspects included Gary Oliva. Oliva was a transient character living in the Boulder area (where the Ramseys lived) who had child sex offences on his slate. Oliva was also found to have a picture of JonBenét Ramsey that he'd cut out of a magazine. Gary Oliva had once tried to choke his own mother and also owned a stun gun. When you tally all this stuff up he was a strong suspect. In the end though the police could find no DNA evidence which linked him to the murder or the Ramsey home.

Another suspect in this case was Gary Hellgoth. Hellgoth was a young electrician who lived near the Ramseys. Apparently he was involved in some sort of property dispute with them. The theory is then that he killed their daughter in revenge. That sounds rather fanciful as a theory but the suspicious thing about Hellgoth is that he killed himself in 1997 - a time when the police were still interviewing suspects and working hard to solve the case. As with Gary Oliva though, no DNA evidence connecting Hellgoth to the murder could be verified.

Other suspects include a local reporter, the housekeeper, and a local Santa Claus impersonator. The JonBenét Ramsey murder is second only to Jack the Ripper when it comes to the number of suspects. In 2006 a man named John Mark Karr claimed - and in disturbing detail too - that he had murdered JonBenét Ramsey. Karr was an unsavoury character with a sexual interest in children - which might explain why he was living in Bangkok. He was flown to Colorado to be questioned in the JonBenét case but it turned out that no DNA evidence connected him to the crime. He was just a sick fantasist wasting police time. He later had a sex change and became a woman.

What makes this sad case especially perplexing is the DNA evidence - which is contradictory, disputed, and in many cases redacted. Private investigators who have studied this case tend to believe in the intruder theory. They think it would have been possible for someone to get into the house through the basement. The Ramsey house was carpeted too so this would have lessened the noise made by footsteps. Others though continue to dispute this theory. The murder of JonBenét Ramsey remains an ongoing investigation but it appears that the real truth has yet to be found. The identity of her killer (or killers?) remains to be officially verified.

CHRISTOPHER REEVE

Christopher Reeve was born in New York in 1962. Reeve was a great student, highly intelligent, and got high grades from a young age. He was also very athletic and participated in all manner of sports. Christopher picked up the acting bug at the age of nine when he appeared in a student play. He attended Cornell University but continued to perform in plays and even went to Europe to study the craft of stage acting in Britain and France. He was very excited too when an agent in New York saw him in a play and offered to represent him. The agent believed that Reeve had the makings of a big star.

Christopher eventually switched to Juilliard School. The Juilliard School is a private performing arts conservatory in New York City. While he was at Juilliard, Christopher Reeve became friends with Robin Williams after they were roomates. Reeve's drama instructor at Juilliard was John Houseman. In his memoir, Christopher Reeve said that Houseman once said to him - "Mr Reeve. It is terribly important that you become a serious classical actor. Unless, of course, they offer you a s***load of money to do something else."

Reeve's first break though was decidedly not classical acting. He appeared in the CBS soap opera Love of Life from 1974 to 1976. He combined the soap opera with appearing in a play on Broadway - which was such an exhausting schedule that he collapsed on stage. The play was a big deal to Reeve because he was appearing with Katherine Hepburn - who became a friend and mentor to him. Reeve blamed his collapse on stage due to the fact that he wasn't getting any sleep and was subsisting on candy bars. Hepburn told him to eat properly and get more sleep - which is sound advice for anyone. Reeve also had a minor part in the 1978 Charlton Heston submarine thriller Gray Lady Down.

In the mid 1970s, a young producer named Illya Salkind and his father and business partner Alexander Salkind embarked on the first lavish big screen Superman film and were considered to be crazy at the time as studios regarded comic book properties to be juvenile and best left on television. The Salkinds secured the twenty-five year rights to Superman on film and television for a modest four million dollars. That was the easy part. Casting and making the movie was a lot more difficult.

Superman made his debut in Action Comics #1 in 1938 and has since had adventures in radio, animation, television and - of course - Tinseltown. The battle to control Superman behind the scenes and the torturous squabbles and feuds over the character and what to do with him have often proved far greater a threat to the Man of Steel than any fictional foe. There is the dubious treatment of Superman creators Jerry Siegel and Joe Shuster, both of whom were elbowed out of the Superman gravy train. In the late seventies it was estimated that Warners had made a billion dollars from their

Superman rights and yet Shuster was legally blind and sleeping on the floor of an apartment in Queens with a broken window while Siegel was earning a paltry $7,500 a year as a clerk.

When Superman was created the publishers had the medium rights to the character. This was not great news for Siegel and Shuster. Four decades later they would still be fighting to get some sort of recognition or money for inventing one of the greatest mythological heroes of all time. Early Superman comics had a monthly circulation of 1.5 million and were essential supplies for the US Marine garrisons at Midway Islands during World War 2. Did you know by the way that Jimmy Olsen and Kryptonite were creations of the radio series and not the comic? Kryptonite was created to make Superman more vulnerable.

There was a radio series where Bud Collyer portrayed Superman in two thousand episodes and then the beautiful forties Superman cartoons created by the Fleischers. Kirk Alyn was the first live action incarnation of Superman in serials but the first Superman movie was a test run for a Superman television series. George Reeves played Superman in the film and also when the character moved to television for the popular Adventures of Superman in the fifties.

The production of 1978's Superman: The Movie had to deal with the eccentricities of nutty Marlon Brando (who at one point suggested that his Jo-El character be depicted as a "bagel"). Brando was signed early - which was a coup for the Salkinds and helped the financing of the picture. Brando earned millions of dollars for a couple of weeks work. He couldn't be bothered to learn his lines for Superman so they had to put them on boards during his scenes so he could read them.

Besides the bonkers Marlon Brando, the production had to cope with cast and crew cheques bouncing (if you worked for the fly by night Salkinds it was best to ask for cash up front), the escalating rift between the producers and their director Richard Donner (Donner was trying to make a great film while the Salkinds were trying to save money), safety concerns (when a crew member died it was hushed up to dampen negative publicity), how to make Superman fly (no one had done anything quite like this at the time), and the endless quest to find someone to fill Superman's red boots.

Many famous actors (Jon Voight, James Caan, Al Pacino Burt Reynolds, Robert Redford, Clint Eastwood, Warren Beatty etc) in Hollywood turned the part of Superman down and they got so desperate in the end they even screentested the handsome dentist of Illya Salkind's wife Skye. The big stars in Hollywood ran for the hills when the Salkinds knocked on their door. They thought that playing Superman would make them a laughing stock and ruin their career. The director Richard Donner wanted to cast Nick Nolte but nothing came of this. "Oh, they were interested in me," said Nolte, "but I turned them off by saying that I would only do it if I could play him as a schizophrenic. That's sabotage."

No one with a big name in Hollywood wanted to play Superman. Caitlyn Jenner, then an athlete named Bruce Jenner, and the singer Neil Diamond even tested for the part because all the actors turned them down. No one had ever made a big budget superhero film at the time. If you mentioned the word 'superhero' the first thing people thought of was the Adam West Batman show or the Spider-Man TV show with Nicolas Hammond in 1977 - a notoriously cheapjack production that never seemed to have any action or villains (which sort of defeated the whole point of doing a live action Spider-Man in the first place). Some shots of a stuntman in an ill-fitting Spider-Man suit endlessly crawling up walls with the aid of an obvious wire was about the best it could offer in the way of spectacle. Superhero films were virtually unheard of because the technology to make them didn't exist.

In the end the Salkinds cast Patrick Wayne, the son of John Wayne, as Superman but Wayne pulled out when his father got ill. Richard Donner wanted to cast an unknown as Superman because that way it would easier for us to simply accept him as Superman. In the pile of photographs of potential Clark Kent actors on his desk was 24 year-old Christopher Reeve. Reeve was 6'4 and certainly looked like Superman. Reeve was flown to London for a screen test and won everyone over. Christopher Reeve was perfect casting and no one ever came close to playing the Man of Steel as well as he did.

The original 1978 Superman probably remains the greatest superhero film ever made. The key to its greatness is that it treats the Superman mythology and character with respect and has a sense of humanity, charm and grandeur that most films in this genre fail to capture or understand. It was developed by Godfather writer Mario Puzo and managed to entice names of the calibre of not only Brando but Gene Hackman. There are three elements in particular vital to the success of the film - although two were happy accidents more than anything.

The first was director Guy Hamilton (best known for four James Bond pictures including Goldfinger) leaving the project and being replaced by Richard (The Omen) Donner, a veteran of film and television who had frequently worked on The Twilight Zone. Donner, who took Superman very seriously, hired Tom Mankiewicz to refine the script and proved to be an inspired choice as director. The second was the casting of Reeve. The final magical component was of course the stirring and majestic Superman theme by John Williams.

The special effects unavoidably look a little rough around the edges these days but the first Superman film is still a lavish and sometimes magical mainstream blockbuster made with much love. One of the great strengths of the film is of course Reeve, who not only looks the part but gives an intelligent performance as Superman, making him somewhat vulnerable and something of an outsider even with all his powers.

One could quibble with Reeve playing Clark Kent like an accident prone imbecile but then some sort of distinction between Kent and Superman has to be made on screen. In the comics Clark Kent is usually as cool as Superman but that probably wouldn't work in a film so well. Reeve's Kent is like an innocent abroad as he struggles to fit into life in the big city. He is from Smallville though and an alien to boot.

Superman and Superman II (which was released in 1980) were shot simultaneously - or at least that was the plan. Richard Donner had completed around 75% of Superman II when he was fired by the Salkinds and replaced with Richard Lester. Lester had to shoot new footage and also reshoot some of Donner's scenes to get his director credit. Lester basically had to direct 51% of the film to be officially credited as the director. So essentially we ended up with two versions of the same film. Donner's not quite completed version and Lester's theatrical version.

The story is the same in both films. Three Kryptonian super villain prisoners - Ursa (Sarah Douglas), Non (Jack O'Halloran) and their leader General Zod (Terance Stamp) - are unwittingly released from "The Phantom Zone" when Superman diverts a missile/bomb into space. As these Kryptonian baddies have the same powers as Superman they soon find that Earth is at their mercy and the fact that Superman - the son of their prosecutor Jor-El - resides on the planet is an added bonus as they can take their revenge. Meanwhile, Clark Kent/Superman, unaware of the great danger about to visit both him and Earth, has fallen in love with Lois Lane and decided to get rid of his powers to live as a human being.

There is - generally - a lot more comedy and sight gags in the Lester Superman II film. The Mount Rushmore gag, more visual jokes during Superman's fight with the villains and also where Zod and his crew wreak havoc in a small dusty nowhere town. One thing I do love about Lester's version though (absent in the Donner cut) is Superman's classic line, "General Zod, would you care to step outside?" Lester's Superman II was the only version we ever got to see for years and generally it's fine. It's funny, the story works, Reeve is great, Stamp is a fine villain, the arc of making Superman mortal is perfect for later building him back up again. By any standards - for its time - Superman II is a terrific sequel and highly satisfying.

Superman II: The Richard Donner Cut is a later 2006 re-edit of the 1980 film Superman II. The decision by the producers not to use Marlon Brando's scenes as Jor-El in the sequel to save money was said to have rankled Donner and one possible explanation for this parting of the ways. In Lester's version Marlon Brando (who had irritated the Salkinds by taking them to court for what he saw as profits owed to him from the first film) was sadly absent to save money and replaced by Susannah York as Superman's mother. So out went a lot of Donner footage and in came new sequences and scenes and much more humour - much to the annoyance of Donner who took Superman far more seriously than Lester and disliked the slapstick/sight gags his replacement added.

Naturally, one of the great things about this new Donner cut of Superman II is that it restores the Marlon Brando as Jor-El "Fortress of Solitude" scenes, which add much more depth and drama to the story and the decision by Superman to become human - and also provide a few explanations for events that were missing in the original version. On the whole and as much as I love the original, Donner's cut is a better film. If he'd been allowed to finish it in the late seventies and shoot everything he'd wanted to it would have been truly amazing. Even this Donner version though, which constitutes about 80% of what he was trying to do with the aid of a screen test and a few new FX shots, is still remarkably good and a great treat for all Superman fans. The restoration of Marlon Brando adds gravitas and drama to the film and there are many wonderful new moments and images rescued from dusty film vaults.

Christoper Reeve won rave reviews for his performance as Superman and became something of an overnight star. He was even a guest on The Muppet Show. In 1980, Reeve appeared in the romantic fantasy film Somewhere in Time with Jane Seymour. The film didn't have much luck because an actor's strike meant that Reeve and Seymour couldn't get out and promote the movie. After his success as Superman, Reeve was very wary of being typecast in action or comic book roles. He said he turned down a lot of action films in order to avoid being pigeon-holed. In 1982 he appeared in the fairly well received mystery film Deathtrap with Michael Caine but then fared less well with Monsignor. Monsignor was a period drama in which Reeve played a dodgy priest in the Vatican. This film was roasted by critics and even Reeve (who was more honest about his films than most actors) later admitted it was terrible.

Next up for Christopher Reeve was Superman III. After the problems that arose with Superman II, producers the Salkinds had a clean slate once again to continue the franchise on their own terms. Lester was hired again and Gene Hackman and Margot Kidder, who had both supported Donner during the Superman II rumpus, were either absent (in the case of Hackman) or reduced to a cameo (Kidder). Lester, who didn't take Superman half as seriously as Richard Donner, once again increased the comic elements and

Superman III also found room for the comedian and comic actor Richard Pryor - who was a huge star at the time - to play a major role in the film.

Superman III opens with a Mack Sennett style slapstick sequence on the streets of Metropolis with an escalating series of comic incidents and accidents that does tend to tip the viewer off to the fact that this is going to be much lighter than Richard Donner's take on Superman. Richard Pryor supplies some funny moments but - as Christopher Reeve later commented - his presence does seem to make Lester look for jokes all the time, like a strange bit where Gorman accidentally skis off the top of the villain's skyscraper wrapped in a pink tablecloth and a scene where Pryor has taken to wearing a giant foam cowboy hat to break into a computer facility.

You do unavoidably sometimes feel like you are watching an early eighties Richard Pryor comedy rather than a Superman film. Perhaps because of this, Superman III subsequently feels less ambitious and a lot dafter than its two predecessors. The best part of the film comes when, after his conscience is given a prod, Superman eventually splits into two different personas and we have an Evil Dark Superman versus Goody two-shoes Clark Kent showdown in an old scrapyard. This is quite an enjoyable sequence and Reeve seems to be enjoying playing a baddie for a change, if only for part of the film.

Superman III did quite well at the box-office but it got terrible reviews. Christopher Reeve was quite disheartened by Superman III as he felt it was too silly and he missed working with Richard Donner. At the time he suggested that Superman III would be his last appearance as this character. Away from the screen, Reeve worked tirelessly for charitable causes and was also a very active outdoors sort of person. He was a pilot and also loved sailing and gliding. He learned to ride horses in 1985 and took part in equestrian events. Reeve was in a relationship with British born modelling executive Gae Exton for ten years and they had two children. He would later marry Dana Morosini and have another child.

Christoper Reeve was not a Hollywood sort of person at all and eventually moved his family out of Los Angeles to Massachusetts.

His older children were born in London and actually lived there when they got older. Reeve would take the Concorde across the Atlantic to see them. In 1984, Reeve enjoyed success when the romantic period drama film The Bostonians (directed by James Ivory) got great reviews. Reeve starred in the film with Vanessa Redgrave. The Bostonians didn't make much money but the artistic success of the film meant a lot to Reeve. The aviation drama The Aviator, in which Reeve played the lead, was less successful though and drew lukewarm reviews.

Reeve was supposed to play Fletcher Christian in The Bounty around this time but pulled out at the last minute because he decided he wasn't right for the part. He was replaced by Mel Gibson. Christopher Reeve also, wisely as it turned, ducked out of a planned cameo in the Salkinds' 1984 Supergirl film. This film got awful reviews and bombed at the box-office. Reeve was definitely struggling to find movie roles that interested him. A project that Reeve wanted to do was Street Smart, which was a script about a magazine reporter in New York who becomes a hot shot after faking a story. However, no one wanted to make Street Smart at the time and Reeve didn't have enough clout to do it himself.

After the relative failures of Superman III and Supergirl, producer Ilya Salkind abandoned plans for another Superman film and sold the Superman rights to low-budget eighties action chancers Cannon Films. Cannon Films enticed (an initially reluctant) Christopher Reeve back in the cape and red underpants by promising to produce Street Smart and allowing Reeve to have story input into Superman IV. Street Smart was directed by Jerry Schatzberg and got pretty decent reviews but it didn't make any money. Cannon didn't market the film very well and never seemed to have much interest in it. It was a means to an end to them as their main objective had been to get Reeve back as Superman.

The notoriously bad Superman IV: The Quest for Peace was directed by Sidney J Furie and released in 1987. This was a famously troubled production that Christopher Reeve later dubbed a "catastrophe". Cannon somehow managed to assemble all the series regulars back - including Reeve and Gene Hackman - and were handed $36 million to make the film by co-producers Warner

Brothers. Unfortunately, Cannon still tried to make the film on the cheap and less than half of the $36 million they were given was actually spent on Superman IV. To make matters worse, a test screening went so badly that Cannon cut over forty minutes from the film until it clocked in at a paltry ninety minutes. Various subplots and supporting characters now made little sense.

The plot has Superman receiving a letter from a small boy who is worried about the threat of nuclear war with tensions in the world rising. After consultations with Lois Lane and the spirits of his Kryptonian ancestors in the Fortress of Solitude, Superman decides he will personally intervene and get rid of all nuclear weapons in the world. He does this by collecting them all in a huge net and throwing it into the sun. Meanwhile, Lex Luthor is sprung from prison by his young nephew Lenny Luthor (John Cryer) and the pair steal a strand of Superman's hair from a science exhibition in Metropolis to create a powerful genetic matrix to attach to a nuclear missile.

When Superman throws the missile into the sun, the mixture of his own DNA and the sun's energy produces - for reasons best known to the writers - a super powered being known as Nuclear Man (Mark Pillow). Despite looking like a reject from Duran Duran, Nuclear Man is as powerful as Superman and soon putting Cannon's cheapskate special effects to the test as the pair do battle in various locations around the world and beyond.

Superman IV's anti-nuclear message and intent to feature a topical plot with political elements is soon negated by the ridiculous Nuclear Man and comic relief from Jon Cryer as Luthor's dim nephew Lenny - who says things like "The Dude of Steel!" whenever Superman shows up. The subplot where The Daily Planet is taken over by the shallow and greedy David Warfield (Sam Wanamaker) is not aided by the savage cuts made to the film. Mariel Hemingway as Lacy Warfield, who takes over as editor of the Daily Planet and develops a romantic interest in Clark Kent, is also rather lost in the edit.

The film's dodgy production values are apparent early on when Superman saves some Soviet Cosmonauts on a space station. The glossy scope and money of the Salkind era films is absent. Superman IV just never quite feels right. Christopher Reeve later trashed the production and talked about how a scene where Superman is supposed to be arriving at the UN building in New York was shot on an industrial park in England with hardly any extras. You really can see the wires in this film and there are some famous gaffs - like the Metropolis subway system having the names of London Underground stations in the background.

When the big smackdown between Superman and Nuclear Man begins to drive the story, the film struggles for two salient reasons. (1) Nuclear Man is a terrible super villain and (2) the special effects are also terrible. When the pair are slugging it out on the Moon they appear to be doing battle in front of a giant black curtain that you half expect a head to pop through. It's a shame really because the film's basic premise had some potential and Christopher Reeve is still a great Superman - not only looking the part but taking the film far more seriously than it really deserves. An early moment where Superman visits his old family farm in Smallville as Clark Kent and can't bring himself to sell it is quite nicely done and gives a very, very brief glimpse of the type of film that Reeve probably wanted Superman IV to be.

Reeve was really angry at Cannon for the way Superman IV turned out. He felt betrayed. The film got terrible reviews. Reeve was definitely retired as Superman now. It's safe to say that none of the actors who have played Superman since Reeve have come anywhere close. 1988 was a fairly average year for Reeve in terms of his career. He had a lead role in the completely forgotten miniseries sequel The Great Escape II: The Untold Story and then had a supporting role in the comedy Switching Channels. Switching Channels was a screwball comedy set in a cable news station. Burt Reynolds and Kathleen Turner were the stars and Reeve had a comic relief supporting part in which he was miscast. Switching Channels got dreadful reviews and Reeve later said that he made a fool of himself in the film.

Christopher Reeve's status, post-Superman, seemed to wane a trifle now because he made a number of television movies. The most notable of these was Bump in the Night in which Reeve played a professor who is a child molester. Reeve was clearly still worried about typecasting and this role certainly went against his Superman image. The Sea Wolf, also made around this time, was a TV movie in which Reeve co-starred with Charles Bronson. Not that Reeve's movie career was over though. He had one of his best roles in the 1993 film Remains of the Day (which was critically acclaimed). Reeve also appeared in Noises Off for Peter Bogdanovich.

Reeve was also in the beloved HBO horror anthology series Tales from the Crypt. The episode he was in was titled What's Cookin'. What's Cookin' was directed by Gilbert Adler and written by AL Katz. In the story, Fred (Christopher Reeve) and Erma (Bess Armstrong) are a couple with a struggling restaurant diner that doesn't make any money. Hardly surprising really as Fred tends to focus on squid themed dishes. No one is interested in his seafood concoctions and their horrible landlord Chumley (Meatloaf) threatens eviction if they don't settle their debts pronto.

An interested observer is a mysterious young man named Gaston (Judd Nelson) who seems to be a sort of homeless busboy. Gaston provides the diner with some steaks that go down a treat and promises to get more. Fred and Erma's diner is soon doing a roaring trade in its rebranded steakhouse mode. The problem? Gaston's much loved steak is actually human flesh and everyone who frequents the diner is now an unwitting cannibal. How will this most unsavoury situation resolve itself?

What's Cookin' is a decent attempt at a very black comedy and probably one of the more memorable Crypt episodes for the outrageous premise if nothing else. The twist at the end is sort of predictable but it works quite well and the story grabs you early on when Gaston bumps off Meatloaf's nagging landlord and uses him for the first of the steaks that pique the tastebuds of the patrons. Christopher Reeve's persona works well here as Fred is just an ordinary well meaning person who somehow ends up in this most grisly and weird state of affairs and Bess Armstrong is well cast too as his long suffering wife Erma. Judd Nelson struggles to be menacing and was obviously never going to end up with many awards on his acting mantelpiece but it's fun anyway to have such a bizarre cultish cast in this one. John Bender and Superman.

In 1995, Reeve was the lead in Village of the Damned, John

Carpenter's remake of the 1960 British film. John Wyndham's story is relocated here to the small coastal village of (naturally) Midwich, California, where a strange, mysterious force/phenomenon knocks everybody inside the village boundary unconscious for several hours, killing two of the inhabitants. Anyone who attempts to enter Midwich immediately collapses inert. When this strange effect finally lifts and the citizens wake-up it soon transpires that nearly all of the local women are now pregnant. The town's doctor, Alan Chaffee (Christopher Reeve), who was away when the incident happened, is bewildered by this mass incubation and government authorities soon begin to show an intense interest in Midwich.

Dr Susan Verner (Kirstie Alley), a secretive epidemiologist from the federal government, arrives to investigate and offers financial rewards for every woman who gives birth. As she continues her research, ten children are born but these aren't ordinary children. They grow at an alarming rate, have silvery white hair, bright green glowing eyes, stick together and are highly intelligent. Village of the Damned is not terribly exciting and a film unlikely to win John Carpenter any new fans, seeming like a modest addition to his CV alongside past glories like Escape From New York, Halloween and The Thing.

In the 1995 television movie Above Suspicion, Reeve played a cop who is paralysed after being shot. Christopher Reeve visited hospitals and learned how to use a wheelchair in preparation for the role. They say that life imitates art and - sadly - this turned out to be the case for Christopher Reeve. On 27 May 1995 in Culpeper, Virginia, six days after the premiere of Above Suspicion, Reeve was competing in a horse riding trial (the Commonwealth Dressage and Combined Training Association Finals) on his horse Buck. In the afternoon event on that day, Reeve had to clear a number of obstacles on the course with Buck. It was basically show jumping.

On the third fence, Christopher's horse declined to jump and suddenly halted. This sudden stop threw Reeve forward off the horse. He landed head-first and crushed his C1 and C2 vertebrae. Upper spinal cord injuries are literally the worst injuries you can suffer. Reeve was flown to the University of Virginia Medical Center. He could not breathe unaided and was paralysed from the neck down. Christopher had no memory of the accident. When he awoke and was told the extent of his injuries he wanted to die but his wife Dana asked him to consent to life saving surgery and at least give it some time to see if he might change his mind in the end. The surgery involved re-attaching Reeve's skull to his spine.

After the surgery, Reeve was confined to a wheelchair and required a straw to suck air because he couldn't breathe on his own. Being paralysed is obviously awful for anyone but it was even worse for Reeve because he was such an active person with so many outdoor pursuits and hobbies. "On a breezy day I'll look at the wind in the trees and realize what a great day it would be to be sailing in Maine," said Reeve. "Or I look at the puffy clouds and think, 'I'd love to be gliding again.' And sometimes I'll say that to somebody nearby. And then I'll let it go."

He adapted to his new circumstances as well as anyone could though and submitted to an exercise routine designed to prevent muscle atrophy. Reeve moved back to New York and required round the clock care. He campaigned for stem cell research and never gave up hope that his condition might be improved or cured one day. He made amazing progress too, even regaining some feeling in his fingers. Reeve got thousands of letters from around the world during this time. This encouraged him to keep on living.

Reeve actually worked too after the accident. He directed the acclaimed HBO movie In the Gloaming and played the lead in a television movie remake of Rear Window. Reeve also made a couple of emotional appearances in the TV show Smallville - which was about a young Clark Kent in the days before he becomes Superman. On October 9, 2004, Reeve attended his son's hockey game. Later that night he went into cardiac arrest after receiving an antibiotic for an infection. He fell into a coma and was taken to Northern Westchester Hospital in New York. Christopher Reeve only had about 20 hours left to live. He died on October the 10th aged 52.

Many stars turned out for Christopher's memorial service and there were tributes from the world of both showbusiness and politics. There was a church service and also a private service at the Juilliard School. In the face of adversity, Reeve had shown courage which was the equal of anything Superman did in comic books. "I'm glad that he is free of all those tubes," said Reeve's mother after his death. Margot Kidder, who played Lois Lane in the Superman films, said - "When you're strapped to someone hanging from the ceiling for months and months, you get pretty darned close. I can't stop thinking about Christopher because he was such a huge part of my life. He was just such a great guy. He was complicated, very smart, really smart, and he knew he'd done something meaningful. He was very aware of that and very happy with that Superman role."

Christopher Reeve was cremated Ferncliff Cemetery, Westchester, and his ashes were scattered by his family. Sadly, Reeve's widow died of cancer only a few years after her husband passes away. Christopher Reeve's children took over the charitable foundations which were set up in Christopher Reeve's name.

JOHN RITTER

John Ritter was born in Burbank, California in 1948. He studied at the University of Southern California and planned to have a career in politics at one point but then he diverted into acting - appearing in many plays as a young man. His breakthrough acting role came when he was cast as Rev. Matthew Fordwick in The Waltons. Ritter would appear in eighteen episodes of this beloved show from 1972 to 1976. The Waltons is a much loved TV series about a family in rural Virginia during the Great Depression and World War II. It was created by Earl Hamner Jr and ran from 1972 to 1981. The Waltons is ultimate comfort blanket television. Trivia - Walton's Mountain in the show, though supposed to be in Virginia, was actually the mountain range just across from the Warner Bros Studios in Los Angeles.

Ritter made guest appearances in many other shows during this time - including Starsky & Hutch and The Streets of San Francisco. Ritter's most famous part though would arrive in 1977 when he was cast in the ABC sitcom Three's Company. This show was an American version of the British sitcom Man About the House. Ritter played Jack Tripper, an aspiring chef who ends up living in an apartment with two women and has to pretend he is gay. This show ran until 1984 and Ritter was also in the spin-off Three's a Crowd. Three's a Crowd ran from 1984 to 1985 and was based on Robin's Nest (which was the British spin-off show from Man About the House).

John Ritter was a very versatile actor in that his stock in trade came in comedic roles but he was perfectly capable of playing dramatic parts. Ritter continued to guest star in numerous other shows and also played the lead in the police comedy/drama show Hooperman. He also appeared in a smattering of movies but he could never quite seem to make the crossover into movie stardom. He probably came the closest when he starred in Skin Deep for Blake Edwards and then starred in the two Problem Child comedy movies. While the Problem Child movies were hardly high art they did make money.

As any horror fan will know, Ritter was also famously in the 1990 miniseries version of Stephen King's IT - where Tim Curry terrified a generation of viewers with his performance as Pennywise the Clown, an inter-dimensional being who preys on the fears of a group of friends from childhood until they band together as adults to tackle him one more time. IT was something of a Waltons reunion as Richard Thomas was one of the adult leads with Ritter.

Ritter's finest hour would come in Sling Blade, a cult 1996 drama written and directed by Billy Bob Thornton- who also plays the memorable central character Karl Childers. Sling Blade begins with the mentally impaired Karl in a psychiatric institution where he has been living since the age of 12 after murdering his mother and her lover - with what he calls a "sling blade". After catching them in a compromising position Karl became confused and believed the man was attacking his mother. When he realised this wasn't the case he then killed both of them. All these years later Karl, regarded as a fairly gentle soul and liked by the hospital staff, is deemed fit for release back into society and, although reluctant after spending most of his life in the institution, must finally leave and fend for himself in the real world. Karl.

Karl is terribly bewildered by life outside (even returning to the institution at one point because he has no idea where to go) but eventually begins the walk proper back to the rural Arkansas town where he was born and raised. Through the kindness of some locals he manages to pick up a basic job repairing lawnmowers and small engines, a craft he picked up in the institution, and is allowed to sleep out the back in the garage of his employer.

His modest new life takes a twist though when he makes a friend in the form of a fatherless young boy called Frank (Lucas Black) and builds a special bond with him despite the initial wariness of Frank's mother Linda (Natalie Canerday) and her friend Vaughan (John Ritter). All are eventually so charmed though by the simple but strangely wise and decent Karl ("I don't think anything bad ought to happen to children. I think the bad stuff should be saved up for the people grown up. That's the way I see it") that he's even invited to live on Linda's property to be close to them. Matters are complicated though by Linda's violent and foul-mouthed redneck boyfriend Doyle (Dwight Yoakam), who doesn't take to Karl at all.

Sling Blade gives John Ritter one of his best ever roles as Vaughan Cunningham, a gay friend of Linda who runs the local store and receives his fair share of abuse from Doyle and plenty of others you suspect around the town. Vaughan is, understandably, rather suspicious about Frank and Linda's new friend at first and decides to keep a close eye on him. There is a great scene with both humour and insight where the pair talk in a diner and Vaughan realises there is much more to Karl than he ever suspected. Karl even draws a parallel between the prejudice faced by him for being mentally challenged and Vaughan for being gay in this particular region of the United States. "The Bible says two men ought not lay together. But I don't reckon the Good Lord would send anybody like you to Hades," says Karl to Vaughan.

In 2003, John Ritter had a recurring role as Zach Braff's dad in Scrubs but his day job (so to speak) at this time was as the lead in the sitcom 8 Simple Rules. Ritter played a parent in the show and his wife was played by Katey Sagal. Kaley Cuoco played one of his kids and there were many familiar guest stars. John Ritter was happy to be in a sitcom because this was sort of where it all started for him and he loved comedic roles. Despite his success those that knew him said he never took acting work for granted. He knew that all actors suffered ups and downs and he was always grateful for new work.

On September 11, 2003, Ritter was in the studio at around 4 in the afternoon on the set of 8 Simple Rules when he began to feel sick. He was sweating and had to go and sit down. Ritter's condition began to get worse though. This was obviously not good at all. It was obvious that something was wrong. Ritter was taken to Providence Saint Joseph Medical Center across the street from the studio and treated for what appeared to be a heart attack. It was more serious than a heart attack though. The diagnosis turned out to be aortic dissection.

Aortic dissection occurs when the innermost layer of the aorta allows blood to flow between the layers of the aortic wall, forcing the layers apart. Aortic dissection can quickly lead to death from insufficient blood flow to the heart or complete rupture of the aorta. Once the diagnosis had been made, Ritter was rushed to surgery. Sadly, the efforts to save him were to no avail. John Ritter died on the operating table at ten in the evening. He was 54 years-old. His death was an almighty shock to the cast and crew on 8 Simple Rules. It was even worse for Ritter's family. They were absolutely devastated. Six hours ago John Ritter was in the studio working on 8 Simple Rules and all of a sudden he was dead. It all happened so quickly.

8 Simple Rules actually went on without Ritter but didn't last very long. His character in the show was killed off through a heart-attack and then the remaining episodes had the family coping with this. There were actually three yet to be transmitted episodes of the show featuring Ritter in the can too. These were shown with a special introduction. John Ritter was married to his second wife when he died. His death was especially tragic because he had young children.

Ritter's family took legal action against the hospital and also his doctor for not diagnosing the aortic dissection. The hospital was not found to be negligent. Ritter had had a medical scan a few years earlier but no heart problems were detected at the time (which, it would appear, was obviously a mistake). If the aortic dissection had been diagnosed he'd probably still be alive today. Ritter's death did at least create publicity for this condition and prevention campaigns in his name were created.

John Ritter was buried at Forest Lawn Memorial Park. His premature death was a great shame because he was a nice man by all accounts and still had so much to give as an actor. The actress Holly Robinson Peete, who was good friends with John Ritter, said - "John was just pure human loveliness. Even though he was such a big star, he always looked you in the eye, connected with you, and made you feel like you're the only one in the room."

The last live action movie John Ritter appeared in, Bad Santa, was released posthumously. John Ritter's father was the country singer and actor Tex Ritter. Tex Ritter died of a heart attack when he was 69 but there is a theory that Tex might actually have suffered an aortic dissection and this condition ran in the family. The Ritter family acting tradition has continued in fresh generations as John's sons Tyler and Jason have both become actors.

SEAN SELLERS

Sean Sellers was born in Corcoran, California, in 1969. In March, 1986, while still a 16 year-old teenager, Sellers killed his mother and stepfather (Vonda and Lee Bellofatto) in Oklahoma City. The victims were asleep at the time. Sellers crept into their room and shot his step-father. He then shot his mother in the face. Sellers then tried to make the house look like it had been robbed. This ruse obviously didn't work. It later transpired that this wasn't the first time Sellers had murdered someone. In 1985 he shot a convenience store clerk who wouldn't sell him any beer.

Sellers was arrested fairly swiftly for the murders of these relatives. At the trial he said he was a Satanist and had become possessed by a demon. His lawyers tried to give the impression that he was addicted to Dungeons & Dragons and that this was a factor in the murders. They were referencing the 'Satanic panic' rumpus surrounding D&D. Dungeons & Dragons is a fantasy tabletop role-playing game (RPG) originally designed by Gary Gygax and Dave Arneson, and first published in 1974. Over fifty million people around the world have played Dungeons & Dragons since it was invented in 1974. The game has though suffered from various controversies in its history.

The Satanic Panic was a 1980s phenomenon in which it was alleged that Satanic ritual abuse was rife in the United States and that young minds were being warped by slasher movies, heavy metal music, and Dungeons & Dragons. The evidence for all this moral outrage? Well, there wasn't any. Not a single allegation of Satanic abuse was substantiated. It's hard to say why Dungeons & Dragons was dragged into this hysteria - although a man named Thomas Radecki had a lot to do with it. Radecki was a psychiatrist who was involved in something called the International Coalition Against Violent Entertainment.

Radecki seemed to develop a strange vendetta against Dungeons & Dragons and claimed that the game was making young people unhinged and even driving them to suicide. No evidence was found for any of these claims. It appears that Radecki got his evidence from a novel called Mazes & Monsters (which was later adapted into a 1982 film with Tom Hanks). The novel was about teens apparently playing 'live' versions of Dungeons & Dragons in dangerous underground tunnels. These tales were urban myths though. People who played Dungeons & Dragons did not take the board game into a cave and then get lost or develop hypothermia. They played the game in their bedrooms, classrooms, or their basements!

The urban myth seemed to derive from a young man named James Dallas Egbert III who went into an underground tunnel to commit suicide but didn't go through with it and then stayed with friends. The press reported though that he'd gone into caves and tunnels to play Dungeons & Dragons - which was patently not true. These days Thomas Radecki is in prison for abusing some of his patients. Another critic of Dungeons & Dragons was Patricia Pulling. When her son shot himself, Pulling claimed that this was a result of a curse her son had received playing Dungeons & Dragons. She set up a group called B.A.D.D. (Bothered About Dungeons & Dragons).

Although Patricia Pullman set herself up as an occult investigator and expert on Dungeons & Dragons her knowledge on the actual game seemed sketchy at best and her claims that there were 300,000 active dangerous Satanists in the United States were ludicrous. Pullman also seemed to think that the Necronomicon (a fictitious 'Demon bible' from the stories of Lovecraft) was a real book used by

Satanists. The campaign seemed especially misplaced because Gary Gygax, the co-creator of Dungeons & Dragons, was a regular at his local church and as far away from a Satanist as you could get.

Regarding the D&D controversies, Gygax said - "Somebody said they threw their copy of D&D; into the fire, and it screamed. It's a game! The magic spells in it are as real as the gold. Try retiring on that stuff." Still, if nothing else, all the hysteria over the game was good for business and simply increased demand for the game. The game was banned from a few school libraries in America but most people seemed to feel the campaign against Dungeons & Dragons was absurd. The legendary FPS video game Doom and the Harry Potter books would later provoke, to varying degrees, similar moral panics. Harry Potter is the most banned book in America, according to the American Library Association. Senior figures in the Catholic Church accused the Potter books of eroding Christianity.

One would think that the best tactic for Sellers' lawyers would have been to plead insanity rather than waffle on about D&D. Sellers later said himself that Dungeons & Dragons played no part in his crimes. Sellers was found guilty of multiple homicides and sentenced to death in 1986. This was a controversial verdict given the young age of Sean Sellers. The sentence was a result of a quirk in Oklahoma law which did not give juries the option of giving a life sentence without the possibility of parole.

They were basically giving the jury two choices. The death penalty OR Sean Sellers probably being released on parole one day while still a relatively young man. The jury evidently felt the latter option was too lenient given the nature of the crimes. Sean Sellers (as ever with murderers and criminals) found God in prison and said he was no longer a Satanist. He appeared on some television shows (The Oprah Winfrey Show and Geraldo) and became something of a true crime celebrity. Sellers got 600 letters a week in prison and even set up his own web page.

There were many appeals against his death sentence and Sellers tried to argue that he suffered from a personality disorder and therefore wasn't of sound mind when he was sentenced. The experts could never quite decide though if Sellers really did have a personality disorder or was simply a very good actor. Sellers claimed that he was abused by his parents (his mother in particular) but there was never too much evidence for this. His family were apparently split on whether Sellers had really changed. Some of his relatives thought he was just faking it to try and get off death row.

Sellers was finally executed by lethal injection in 1999 at the age of 29. He sang Christian music as his execution loomed and for his last meal on death row he had Chinese food (egg rolls, sweet and sour shrimp, batter-fried shrimp). Sellers remains the only person executed in the United States for a crime committed under the age of 17 since the reinstatement of the death penalty in 1976.

ANNA NICOLE SMITH

Anna Nicole Smith was born Vickie Lynn Hogan in Houston in 1967. She left school when she was fourteen and got a job in a fried chicken fast food place - Jim's Krispy Fried Chicken - in Mexia. Anna got married to another employee there when she was about 17. The marriage didn't last but it did produce a son named Daniel. Anna Nicole Smith became a stripper next and then eventually a Playboy model. You could say she was sort of like the 1990s version of Jayne Mansfield in the end. Anna Nicole was a bit of a hustler and a good self-publicist. She wanted fame and wealth and her idol was Marilyn Monroe.

Anna Nicole Smith looked like a cartoon character sex symbol and her life was like a soap opera that no scriptwriter could have made up. It wasn't just Playboy shoots. She was photographed for fashion magazines and even had a movie career. She was in The Hudsucker Proxy and the third Naked Gun movie with Leslie Nielsen. As you might imagine, there were a lot of jokes in the Naked Gun movie about Smith's, er, assets. Smith played Tanya Peters, a nurse at a fertility clinic.

Anna Nicole Smith was also in To the Limit with John Travolta. On television she appeared in Veronica's Closet and Ally McBeal. As if that wasn't enough, Smith also appeared in a music video for Bryan

Ferry. Suffice to say, she did her level best to make the most of her window of fame. While she was too limited a thespian to have a long screen career she took advantage of her Playboy fame to have a decent little run in the world of acting.

The most infamous part of the Anna Nicole Smith story began in 1991 when she met the billionaire oil tycoon J. Howard Marshall at a strip club. Marshall was smitten with Anna Nicole and asked her to have lunch with him. He wanted to marry her. Nothing wrong with that you might say. There was only one problem. Marshall was 86 years-old. Anna Nicole Smith was in her twenties. Three years later the pair got married. The wheelchair bound Marshall was nearly 90 when they tied the knot.

Anna Nicole Smith was adamant that she had not married Marshall for his money. That had nothing to do with it at all. She had married him purely out of love. Pull the other one Anna Nicole. It's got bells on. It's probably fairly safe to say that Anna Nicole Smith would not have been marrying J. Howard Marshall if he was penniless and living in a garden shed. You can see what her calculation was. I just have to look after this old geezer for a couple of years and then once he shuffles off this mortal coil I'll inherit his billions. What could possibly go wrong?

After the wedding, J. Howard Marshall lasted about thirteenth months before he passed away in 1995. Doubtless he died happy in the pneumatic bosum of Anna Nicole Smith. Now came the inevitable mud-slinging battle for the old man's money. Marshall had not named Anna Nicole Smith in his will but Anna Nicole wasn't willing to let a small detail like that deny her the billions her late husband had left. Marshall's family and the former Playboy Playmate went to court in a case that lasted ten years. Anna Nicole won in the end but unresolved issues then necessitated more court drama so her victory was snatched away. Anna Nicole would not live long enough to see this case finally resolved.

Anna Nicole Smith claimed that her late husband had verbally promised her half of his estate. She would say that wouldn't she? Half of J. Howard Marshall's estate amounted to $1.6 billion. Anna Nicole, with no self-awareness whatsoever, was basically saying -

look, I'm being reasonable and I'm not greedy. I'm willing to share. I only want $1.6 billion! You will not be surprised to hear that Marshall's family dismissed this claim and so the wearisome legal battle commenced. At one point Anna Nicole was awarded about $400 million in court and then this was reduced to $88 million. The case dragged on though with no clear conclusion. Anna Nicole certainly wasn't going to settle for $88 million given that her late husband of thirteen months was worth billions. She wanted a bigger slice of the pie.

As she got a bit older and put on weight, Anna Nicole found that the model and film work began to dry up. Her telephone did not ring as often as it used to. She had a decent comeback though in 2002 with The Anna Nicole Show. This was a (rather contrived) reality show on the E! network which followed her around with her entourage. In the series Anna Nicole gives one the impression that she is struggling financially after all the costly legal battles in the ongoing fight to get her manicured mitts on her late husband's money. The main supporting character in the show is Anna Nicole's shrewd and grumpy lawyer Howard K. Stern. Her publicity shy son Daniel pops up now and again to be comically embarrassed by his larger than life mother.

In 2004, Anna Nicole made an an eccentric appearance at the American Music Awards and seemed to be drunk. She was by now addicted to various pills and medications. In 2006, Anna Nicole Smith gave birth to a daughter named Dannielynn. The father was presumed to be her lawyer Howard K. Stern - to whom Anna Nicole had grown close. Howard K. Stern made no attempts to dissuade anyone from thinking he was the father. In fact, he strongly suggested he WAS the father.

On September 10, 2006, Anna Nicole Smith suffered a devastating and tragic blow when her 20 year-old son Daniel died through a combination of methadone and antidepressants. Daniel was actually visiting his mother and Dannielynn in the hospital at the time of his death. Anna Nicole had always been very close to Daniel and never recovered from the grief and pain of his passing. It is said that when they buried Daniel she was so distraught she tried to climb into the grave with him.

Not long after this tragedy, Anna Nicole had a 'commitment' ceremony with Howard K. Stern. It was sort of like a marriage ceremony but without the legal stuff. Things got really weird now because Smith and Stern were holed up in the Bahamas. The main reason for this is that they didn't want a paternity test for her daughter Dannielynn. A photographer named Larry Birkhead was now claiming that he, and NOT stern, was the father of Dannielynn. Birkhead was perfectly willing to go to court to prove this.

A number of men had come out of the woodwork claiming to be the father of Anna Nicole's daughter. The most bizarre of these was Zsa Zsa Gabor's husband Frederic Prinz von Anhalt - who claimed to have had a ten-year affair with her. Stern was still acting as if he was the father though. Anna Nicole was, in a childlike sort of way, trying to hide from all of this. She never managed to regain any mental stability after the death of her beloved son.

Anna Nicole Smith was eventually evicted from her house in the Bahamas and ended up in Florida. On February 8, 2007, Smith was found unresponsive at the Seminole Hard Rock Hotel & Casino and died in hospital. She died from an overdose of a battery of prescription drugs. Nothing illegal was found it her system and it was judged to be an accident rather than a suicide. A case of misadventure, as they say. Anna Nicole was zonked out at the end of her life. The death of Daniel was so painful she could barely face reality anymore.

There was a bit of a battle between relatives and Stern over where to bury Anna Nicole but in the end she was buried in the Bahamas with her son. She had died five months after Daniel. Anna Nicole Smith left just $1 million when she died. She never got any of J. Howard Marshall's billions in the end. Believe it or not, the estates of Marshall and Anna Nicole Smith carried on fighting in court until 2011 - long after Anna Nicole and J. Howard Marshall were dead. A Chief Justice in the case compared the depressing and seemingly endless legal saga to Bleak House by Charles Dickens.

Anna Nicole had named Daniel as her beneficiary in her will. Daniel had obviously passed away so Howard K. Stern took control of Anna Nicole's estate. Dannielynn, the infant daughter of Anna Nicole, was next in line though after Daniel and if any money was extracted from the Marshall court case then Dannielynn would get that too. If you were being VERY cynical you could see then why Howard K. Stern was happy to be thought of as Dannielynn's father. A court case and DNA test though established that Larry Birkhead was Dannielynn's father and so he got custody of the child.

Anna Nicole Smith may be gone but she still continues to abound in popular culture. There has been a Netflix documentary about her and even an opera based on her life. As for Smith's infant daughter Dannielynn, well, she's now called Dannielynn Birkhead and lives with her father in Louisville, Kentucky. She attends high school and is often seen at the Kentucky Derby with her dad. Larry Birkhead posts updates on his daughter's life and said she's preparing for college and is interested in forensics and photography.

It was sometimes wrongly reported that Dannielynn Birkhead was one of the richest kids in America but this wasn't the case at all. None of J. Howard Marshall's billions were given to the estate of Anna Nicole Smith. The assumption that Dannielynn inherited a fortune is simply not true. Dannielynn only got the money from her mother's estate and while that was a nice sum it wasn't anything which would land her on the rich list. Not that Dannielynn seemed too bothered anyway. Dannielynn Birkhead is very happy living out of the spotlight and says she has no interest in being an actress or model like her mother. A few years ago, in tribute to her mother, Dannielynn wore the same pink hat to the Kentucky Derby that her mother once wore to this event.

SAMANTHA SMITH

Samantha Smith was born in Maine in 1972. Her father was an academic and her mother was a social worker. When she was ten years-old, Yuri Andropov became the new leader in the Soviet Union. In these tense Cold War times there was always some unease in the United States when someone new took over in the Soviet Union because they didn't quite know what to expect. Given that the Soviet Union had even more nuclear weapons than the United States the thought of someone dangerous or crazy getting the keys to the Kremlin was nightmarish indeed. The world situation was tense at the time because the Soviet–Afghan war was three years old and showed no sign of ending.

Like the Russian invasion of Ukraine many years later, the Soviet–Afghan war had become a proxy war (albeit a more covert proxy war) with Western nations like the United States lending military and financial assistance to those fighting the Soviets. The Soviet Union, in both its economy and military, was much more powerful than modern day Russia. The Soviet bloc numbered 483 million and Moscow also controlled the industrial might of Eastern Europe. A lot of the Western unease about Yuri Andropov was because he was known as "The Butcher of Budapest" for his role in the 1956 Hungarian Uprising.

This uprising was crushed when Moscow sent the tanks and army in. Andropov was the Soviet ambassador to Hungary at the time and it was him who suggested that that the Kremlin should send the military to quash this revolution. In 1982, Samantha Smith saw an article in Time magazine about Yuri Andropov taking over in Moscow and asked her father why they didn't just write a cordial letter to Andropov asking him if he planned to avoid war. Samantha's father pondered the question for a moment and suggested to his daughter that she should drop a line to Andropov. So Samantha went right ahead and did that. Her letter was as follows...

Dear Mr. Andropov,

'My name is Samantha Smith. I am 10 years old. Congratulations on your new job. I have been worrying about Russia and the United States getting into a nuclear war. Are you going to vote to have a war or not? If you aren't please tell me how you are going to help to not have a war. This question you do not have to answer, but I would like it if you would. Why do you want to conquer the world or at least our country? God made the world for us to share and take care of. Not to fight over or have one group of people own it all. Please lets do what he wanted and have everybody be happy too.'
To the amazement of Samantha's family, she actually got a reply from Yuri Andropov. Andropov compared Samantha to Becky in

Tom Sawyer and promised her that no one in the Soviet Union wanted a war with the United States. He said that people in the Soviet Union knew all too well about the horrors and hardships of war from being attacked by Nazi Germany forty odd years ago. He reminded Samantha that the Soviet Union and the United States were allies in the defeat of Hitler's plans for world domination. Andropov obviously didn't mention the fact that the Soviet Union had then occupied Eastern Europe and turned the countries there into puppet states of Moscow.

Andropov invited Samantha to visit the Soviet Union in the summer to see for herself that the Soviets were a friendly peaceful people. So that's exactly what Samantha did. In July, Samantha flew to Moscow with her parents and spent two weeks in the Soviet Union. She visited Leningrad and then stayed at an Artek pioneer camp on the Black Sea. This was a youth organisation. Samantha slept in a dorm with Soviet kids and made some new friends. Samantha was supposed to sleep in quarters assigned to dignitaries but she insisted on bunking with the other kids and didn't want to spend the trip in hotels. She wanted to meet real people - that was the point of the trip.

Samantha became an instant celebrity in the Soviet Union and her trip was covered by the state media. She was lauded as a courageous young peace activist. I suppose you could say this was all good propaganda for the Soviets in a sense as they were able to show the best side of themselves to Smith's family and carefully stage manage her trip but it was hard to be too cynical about the well meaning Samantha Smith because she was at least showing that kids were alike all over. Samantha's message was that rival nations with different systems should somehow learn to trust one another more. A good way to start that process was for their young people to meet each other.

Samantha never actually met Andropov during the trip because he was ill. Andropov had kidney failure in 1983 and was bedridden in hospital until his death in 1984. Back in the United States, Samantha had also become a celebrity. She even appeared on The Johnny Carson Show. Given that she was only ten years-old, Samantha gave an impressive performance on the show. She was relaxed and funny.

Samantha told Johnny all about her strange but exciting trip to the Soviet Union. Samantha had become what you might describe as a Cold War icon. A famous cartoon by Don Wright of The Miami Herald depicted two nuclear warheads facing one another with a little girl daintily jumping from one to the other. That was a perfect image for what Samantha Smith had done. She navigated an impossible divide and enchanted the enemy in the process.

Samantha Smith reminded people a bit of The Exorcist era Linda Blair in that she was an articulate, cute kid with a big smile. Samantha was dubbed 'America's youngest diplomat' and was even invited to Japan to meet the Prime Minister. Samantha had a rather ingenious plan for world peace. She said leaders should have to send their grandchildren to live in other countries for part of the year. As she reasoned, who would bomb a nation where the leader's grandchild was living? I suppose one could say that Smith was sort of like a less intense American version of Greta Thunberg. Both were child activists with their hearts in the right place who got a lot of media and press.

In 1984, Samantha Smith hosted a Disney special about politics and even interviewed some of the candidates for the Democratic nomination. Samantha was an absolute natural when it came to presenting and interviewing people. She was intelligent, curious, and funny in the Disney political special. It could be that television presenting might well have been her vocation in the end. She was a good public speaker too - especially when talking to other kids.

Samantha Smith also guest starred in Charles in Charge (a sitcom that ran from 1984 to 1990). Samantha was the envy of her friends when she appeared in Charles in Charge. She had to promise them she'd get the autograph of its star Scott Baio (who was a big pin-up at the time and famous for Happy Days). In the episode of Charles in Charge, Samantha played a Duran Duran obsessed girl who comes over for a slumber party. Given that she'd never acted before, Smith delivers her lines in a pleasantly natural way and clearly has a knack for comedy. You can't imagine Greta Thunberg doing a funny slumber party cameo in Charles in Charge! Trivia - two of the other girls at the slumber party with Samantha Smith are the famous gymnast Julianne McNamara and a very young Christina Applegate.

Samantha, unwittingly, also had a close brush with the unwelcome side of fame around this time when she attracted the attention of Robert John Bardo. Bardo was the lunatic who later murdered the actress Rebecca Schaeffer in Los Angeles by shooting her dead on her doorstep. Bardo actually went to Maine looking for Samantha Smith but was detained by police and sent home. In 1985, Samantha dipped a more permanent toe in the world of acting when she was asked to appear in a new action/drama show called Lime Street for ABC. Lime Street starred Robert Wagner as a widowed man who investigates insurance claims while looking after his two daughters. Samantha accepted the offer to appear in Lime Street and took the role of the elder daughter Elizabeth. It is said that Robert Wagner had the idea to cast Smith after being impressed with one of her chat show appearances.

Samantha filmed the pilot and three episodes of Lime Street before taking a well earned break. She actually had to go to London to shoot some scenes so there was a lot of travel involved. On August 25, 1985, Samantha and her 45 year-old father Arthur were on the last leg of flying back to Maine when their commuter plane struck some trees attempting to land at Lewiston-Auburn Regional Airport. The plane failed to clear a wooded hill and came down about half a mile from the airport it was trying to land in. The wreckage was strewn across a field and the emergency services had to put the flames out before they could inspect what was left of the plane. Tragically, all eight passengers - including Samantha Smith and her father - were killed when the plane crashed. Samantha was just thirteen years-old at the time of her death.

An investigation into the crash apportioned no blame to the pilots. It was a rainy night and something just went wrong. A thousand people turned up for Samantha's memorial service at St. Mary's Roman Catholic Church. There were messages of condolence from both President Ronald Reagan and Mikhail Gorbachev. "You should know millions of mothers and fathers and kids back in Russia share this tragic loss," said Gorbachev. Gorbachev's tribute was read at the memorial by his emissary Vladimir Kulagin. Kulagin worked at the Soviet Embassy in Washington and was given clearance by the State Department to speak at the memorial.

Samantha's mother Jane was comforted by the actor Robert Wagner at the service. Jane had lost her daughter and husband in the plane crash. She was absolutely devastated. William Prebble, Samantha's school advisor, said at the memorial service - "This little girl did things that governments don't have the power or the will to do." Samantha and her father were cremated and their ashes laid to rest at Estabrook Cemetery, Amity, Maine.

The Soviet Union issued a commemorative stamp with Samantha's likeness after her death. A monument was built to her at the pioneer camp she visited (though heartless thieves later stole this monument for scrap metal when the Soviet Union collapsed). Ships, diamonds, schools, and even asteroids have been named after Samantha Smith. Who knows what she might have done had she lived? A Hollywood star? Television presenter? Writer? Activist? Become the first female President of the United States? We'll never know now.

They tried to continue Lime Street after Samantha died but after eight episodes realised this was a waste of time. Trivia - Samantha actually inspired the plot of Superman IV: The Quest For Peace (where a kid writes to Superman asking him why he doesn't get rid of nuclear weapons). On the 30th anniversary of Samantha's death, Maine State Museum hosted an exhibition based on artefacts from her life. She was gone but certainly not forgotten. To this day, at her old school Manchester Elementary, kids are still taught about the short but eventful life of Samantha Smith and her inspiring peace mission at the height of the Cold War.

MARK SPEIGHT

Mark Speight was born in Seisdon, Staffordshire in 1965. His mother was an art teacher so it was perhaps no surprise that he was eventually drawn to art as a career. He left school at sixteen to go to an art school. Speight's ambition was to be a cartoonist. He ended up though taking an unexpected detour when he became a television presenter on the BBC kids show SMart after he attracted the attention of the BBC when he had a job painting a TV studio. That was what you might call a lucky break but Speight was clearly a natural when it came to TV presenting.

SMart was a children's art show sort of in the vein of Take Hart (a popular kids art show with Tony Hart which ran for many years on the BBC). SMart even featured Morph - a stop-motion clay character made famous through Take Hart. SMart was also inspired by the success of the ITV kids art show Art Attack with Neil Buchanan. SMart began in 1994 and ran for many years. During his time on the show Speight's co-presenters included Zoe Ball and Kirsten O'Brien. Speight, with his spiky blond hair and enthusiastic bubbly personality, took to television presenting like a duck to water and became a familiar face to a generation of kids. Speight loved the fact too that he was doing something educational and encouraging a love for art in young people.

Speight also appeared on the Saturday morning show Scratchy & Co. and the kids game show See It Saw It. If you were a child watching television in late 1990s Britain it was impossible not to encounter Mark Speight. He was all over the place. It was while working on See It Saw It that Speight met Natasha Collins. Natasha Collins was born in Luton in 1976. She played a jester to Mark's king on See It Saw It. Speight and Collins became a couple in the end and eventually moved in together.

Natasha's ambition was to be a serious actress but she'd ended up in kids TV trying to pay the bills. She was in another kids show called Chucklevision (which featured that legendary comic duo The Chuckle Brothers) but also had a few 'proper' if small acting gigs in The Tenth Kingdom and Real Women. Natasha Collins also done some theatre and corporate videos. Natasha was actually cast in the (seemingly neverending) Channel 4 teen soap Hollyoaks at one point but then had to pull out of the show due to a bad car crash which left her in a coma. That was a very unlucky break because Hollyoaks was the sort of acting work that Natasha craved.

Natasha Collins was in hospital for a long time after the car crash and suffered seizures afterwards. This put an end to her immediate acting ambitions but she became very close to Mark Speight during this time. Mark Speight continued to be a busy man. He did art workshops for children, lots of charity work, and even appeared in

Christmas pantomime.

By 2008, Speight and Natasha Collins were living together in a flat in St John's Wood in London. St John's Wood is famous for being the home of Lord's Cricket Ground and Abbey Road Studios. On the afternoon of 3 January 2008, the 42 year-old Speight, who was clearly in some distress, phoned for an ambulance. He said he needed assistance fast.

Natasha Collins was unconscious in the bath of their flat. In fact, she was dead at the age of 31. Speight and Natasha Collins had spent the previous evening on something of a bender - to put it mildly. They had taken huge quantities of cocaine, drunk vodka and champagne, and then used sleeping pills. At some point Natasha, for some reason, had got up to take a bath and then then fallen asleep and passed out. The hot water from the bath had scalded her body and left extensive burns.

What had really killed Natasha though was the cocaine binge. Natasha had ingested a 'lethal' amount of cocaine. It was also discovered in the post-mortem that she had a hole in her nose - which is obviously a tell tale sign of persistent heavy cocaine use. The devastated Mark Speight was actually arrested at this point. Not just for supplying drugs but also - for a brief time at least - on suspicion of murder. The police had to establish if there was any foul play in this death and that obviously entailed talking to Mark Speight. This was certainly a bizarre breaking story. Not only was this famous children's presenter a cocaine fiend he was now suspected of killing his girlfriend.

Speight was eventually cleared of any suspicion that he had been involved in the death of Natasha Collins. No charges were brought against him either for the fact that his flat the previous night apparently contained more cocaine than a Mexican drug cartel factory. Natasha's death was simply an overdose and accident as a consequence of taking too many drugs. The coroner believed that Natasha Collins may have had a heart problem too - which contributed to her death. The heart problem was presumably connected to taking all of this cocaine. Mark Speight was now a ruined man. He quit his TV show SMart and sunk into a heavy depression. He couldn't imagine life without Natasha - to whom he had been engaged. He moved in with Natasha's mother at this time. At the inquest into Natasha's death, Mark Speight was a gaunt and haunted figure and could barely summon any words.

On the 7th of April, about three months after the death of Natasha Collins, Mark Speight was due to meet Natasha's mother in Convent Garden but he never turned up. He had also missed a therapy session. The next day he was reported missing. CCTV was then found of Speight using a cash machine and boarding a train on the Waterloo line but the trail went cold after this. In all, Mark Speight would be missing for six days before a tragic discovery was made.

Railway workers found Mark's body in MacMillan House near London's Paddington Station on April the 13th. Mark Speight had hung himself. It is believed that he used a fire escape to get to the secluded spot where he killed himself. Speight left two suicide notes. In his suicide notes he said he could not contemplate life without Natasha so had decided to end it all. His death was a great shock to the BBC and all the people who had watched his shows. Kirsten O'Brien, who was best mates with Speight and co-presented with him, had the unenviable task of announcing his death to an audience of children on CBBC.

Mark Speight's funeral was held on 28 April at St Michael and All Angels' Church in Tettenhall. The theme from SMart was played during the funeral. Speight's father said his son had been a Pied Piper figure who took children on a magical art adventure. Hundreds of people turned out for his funeral and many children contacted the BBC to send their condolences. At the funeral, Mark Speight's father said of his son - "You leave here with the adoration of those 7,000 children that emailed the BBC and who miss you today - sleep well in eternity, you have earned your rest."

Carmen Collins, the mother of Natasha Collins, later told the newspapers that Mark Speight had once confided to her that he wished he'd never gone into television because there were too many drugs. Carmen Collins said there was a 'cocaine culture' at the BBC - even in children's television - and that this had destroyed her late daughter's life. "In hindsight, I'd love it if Natasha had chosen to go into teaching like her sister and not into TV. But she had this dream of being an actress and the drug culture in the industry killed her."

Mark Speight's father set up an art foundation charity in his son's memory in 2008. The aim of the foundation is to create as many artistic and creative workshops for children as possible. That was certainly something that the late Mark Speight would have loved and heartily approved of. SMart only ran for one more season after the death of Mark Speight. The show, including repeats, was suspended when he died but one had one last season on CBBC until it ended in 2009. SMart just wasn't the same without Mark Speight. You could say then that the show was retired in his honour.

REEVA STEENCAMP

Reeva Steenkamp was born in Cape Town in 1983. She studied law at university and then became a fashion model. Reeva won beauty contests, was the face of Avon in South Africa, and did many commercials. She was also a television presenter. South African FHM readers voted her one of the sexiest women in the world and Reeva was also a familiar face on the high society party scene and celebrity red carpets. Reeva was also a reality television star too. Reeva Steenkamp was a young woman who seemed to have just about everything. She was no stranger to adversity though. She broke her back falling off a horse when she was younger and had to learn to walk all over again.

In 2012, Reeva began dating Oscar Pistorius - the world famous Olympic and Paralympic athlete. Pistorius had both his legs amputated when he was an infant but his feats as an athlete with aritifical legs and blades (hence his nickname Blade Runner) had won him admirers around the world. At the 2012 London Olympics, Pistorius became the first amputee runner to compete at an Olympic Games. Pistorius also carried the flag for South Africa in the games. Oscar Pistorius was one of the most famous people in South Africa and someone who seemed to project a positive image for the country. That was all about to change in shocking fashion.

Reeva and Pistorius lived together in Pretoria. They lived in the gated, high-security community of Silver Woods Country Estate - a swanky place where you had to have a lot of money to live. It was the sort of place where rich people in South Africa go to avoid crime - a sort of protective bubble with security guards and cameras. South Africa tends to rank highly on the list of nations with the worst crime rate and so Silver Woods was appealing to those who tend to have anxiety about such things. Silver Woods was even surrounded by an electrified fence. Oscar owned the house in the community. He and Reeva had only been dating for a few months.

In the early morning of Thursday, 14 February 2013, Reeva was in the bathroom of their home. They had both apparently struggled to sleep that night due to the heat and humidity. At some point the police were contacted and told that Oscar had shot his girlfriend. They knew full well that the person being spoken of was Reeva Steencamp. Pistorius had phoned for an ambulance and then carried Reeva downstairs in bloodied towels. A doctor (who was a neighbour of the couple) tried to lend assistance but it was too late. Reeva's injuries were too severe. She was dead at the age of 29.

Oscar Pistorius had fired four shots through the bathroom door - three of which struck Reeva. One of them was a head shot - so her chances of survival were almost zero. Her skull was fractured by this bullet. At the trial it was revealed that Pistorius used a special kind of ammunition which opened up upon contact. Suffice to say, these bullets were deadly and very nasty. Pistorius, by all accounts, had always been obsessed with guns. One bullet had struck Reeva in the hip and another went through a finger into her arm. The door to the bathroom had been smashed in with a cricket bat. Oscar Pistorius said he had done this to check on who was in the bathroom after the shots because the door was locked.

Reeva was cremated at Victoria Park crematorium in Port Elizabeth. Her family were devastated and angry. As for Oscar Pistorius, he was arrested and charged with murder. The trial began on 3 March 2014 in the High Court in Pretoria. Oscar Pistorius claimed that he had shot Reeva because he thought she was an intruder. He believed that a stranger had got into their home. Pistorius said that he thought Reeva was in the bedroom when he heard what sounded like an intruder in the bathroom. He felt vulnerable because he wasn't wearing his artificial legs. Oscar alleged that he grabbed his pistol in the dark (he was too fearful to put the lights on) and judged that an intruder was hiding in the bathroom. He was terrified because he believed that both he and Reeva might be killed by this criminal.

Oscar Pistorius then said that he fired some shots at the bathroom door and shouted for Reeva to call the police. It was only when he checked the bedroom and saw that Reeva wasn't there that it dawned on him that she might have been the person in the bathroom (which tragically turned out to be the case). So this was basically the defence of Oscar Pistorius. It was all a dreadful accident. He was simply trying to protect Reeva by dealing with what he thought was an intruder out to rob and harm them. The defence case was perhaps somewhat helped by the fact that South Africa is a notoriously violent country where murders abound at an alarming rate. Many people own guns for their own protection and Pistorius was one of them.

The legal team of Oscar Pistorius argued that he had acted in self-defence that night and the last thing he would have done was intentionally harm Reeva. They believed he should only be charged with culpable homicide (which means that you killed someone but didn't mean to do so - basically manslaughter). Pistorius gave an emotional performance during the trials and often sobbed. When the court was shown pictures of Reeva's head injuries, Oscar vomited into a bucket. Were the tears though for Reeva or himself?

The prosecution put forward a very different scenario for what happened on that tragic night. They argued that Pistorius had deliberately shot Reeva after an argument and then pretended it had been an accident. The original lead detective in this case was Hilton Botha - until he was removed due to troubles of his own. Botha had previously arrested Pistorius over an alleged assault charge (this was on another woman - not Reeva). The charges were dropped in the end though. Botha believed Pistorius was guilty of murder. Of that he had no doubt.
Botha was the first police detective on the scene when Reeva was shot and he was immediately suspicious of Oscar. He noted that Pistorius had washed Reeva's blood off his hands. He certainly didn't

believe Oscar's claim that he thought Reeva was a burglar. Botha said that made no sense because the position of the body and entry points of the bullets (they hit her from the right hand side) suggested Reeva was crouched behind the door when she was shot. This indicated that she was hiding or taking refuge rather than using the toilet or wash basin. It also transpired that Reeva had taken her phone into the bathroom. Why had she done this?

Botha also believed that the angle (in terms of their height) of the bullets indicated that Oscar was wearing his artificial limbs when he shot Reeva. Oscar claimed during the trial that he was on his stumps when he fired the shots and this was part of the reason why he felt vulnerable and scared. The trial and ballistics evidence seemed to indicate that Oscar WASN'T wearing his artificial legs when he shot Reeva but then this didn't explain how he managed to smash down a door with a cricket bat (which would have been very difficult to do on his stumps).

Botha resigned after he was dropped from the case. He believes he was drummed out of the police because he didn't believe the story of Oscar Pistorius. Botha felt that Oscar's story was fanciful because the most reasonable course of action in that scenario (an intruder in one's house) would be to grab Reeva and then flee for help. Oscar clearly never did this. Why would you shoot four gun shots at a bathroom door when you can't see who is on the other side? Even if Oscar was telling the truth, it still betrayed a ruthless quality - the fact that he blasted the door with gun shots and knew full well that he might killing whoever was inside.

Pistorius claimed that he suspected an intruder because he found an open window. Botha said though that he had tested this window with police officers and they determined it would have been impossible for an adult to climb through it because it was too small. At the trial, text messages between Reeva and Oscar were revealed. The vast majority were friendly and normal but about 10% were not. In one of them Reeva told Oscar she was scared of him and the rages he could get into.

The defence pointed out though that the vast majority of the texts were loving and that Reeva had even sent Oscar an affectionate text on the day of her death. The prosecution argued that neighbours heard screams the night of Reeva's death which could be interpreted as a woman screaming for help. The defence argued though that screams would have been inaudible to neighbours coming from the bathroom and that any noises heard were from Oscar shouting for help when he deduced that Reeva had been shot. The defence also said that Oscar had a high pitched voice when he shouted or got emotional and so could have been mistaken for a woman screaming.

At the trial the prosecution said that Pistorius had two charges in his past for reckless use of a gun. A former girlfriend said he carried a gun around at all times and once fired it angrily through the sunroof on his car when he got annoyed because some cops had pulled him over. Pistorius had also fired someone else's gun at a restaurant. This happened only a few weeks before the death of Reeva Steencamp. Much was made of the fact that Pistorius suffered from anxiety and so got into a panic when he thought there might be an intruder.

One problem though was that the rich gated community he lived in had high security and no history of home invasions or crime. If you were a burglar or rapist (and the defence of Pistorius was basically that he feared a thief or rapist was in his home) this was one of the last places you'd choose to operate because of the higher risk of being caught. It wouldn't make sense to target a place like this (though such a place, with its well-heeled inhabitants, would potentially provide some rich pickings).

The trial of Oscar Pistorius was the most watched celebrity court case since OJ Simpson. People from around the world avidly followed it on news channels. Under the South African system there was no jury but simply a judge with two assessors. The judge would have to decide the fate of Pistorius. What this case came down was whether or not the evidence suggested Pistorius had not intended to kill Reeva and made a bad and fatal mistake or whether or not he had a dark side and had shot her on purpose.

The defence team had the easier task in court because they had to argue that this was a strange and tragic accident. That was slightly easier than trying to prove Oscar Pistorius was a killer who had snapped and shot Reeva dead in brutal fashion. There was speculation that Oscar might have killed Reeva because he found out she was seeing an old boyfriend but none of this was proven. On 12 September 2014, Oscar Pistorius was found not guilty of murder, but guilty of culpable homicide. He was sentenced to five years in prison but in December 2015, the Supreme Court of Appeals overturned the culpable homicide verdict and found Pistorius guilty of murder.

In 2016 he was sentenced to six years in prison - which created a rumpus because that was well short of the minimum sentence for murder. On 24 November 2017, the Court of Appeal extended Oscar Pistorius's jail term to 13 years and five months with the possibility of parole from 2023. Oscar Pistorius was denied parole in 2023 but he will up for parole again in 2024. Reeva's mother June told the media that Pistorius was neither rehabilitated or remorseful. She would clearly like him to stay in prison for longer.

PATRICK SWAYZE

Patrick Swayze was born in Texas in 1952. His mother was a dancer, choreographer, and dance instructor and so Swayze was always interested in dancing and studied ballet for a time as a young man. He could also sing too and co-wrote the song She's Like the Wind. Patrick Swayze was certainly versatile though because he also studied martial arts and made a convincing action hero in movies like Point Break and Road House. Swayze was a good actor too and if you gave him a purely dramatic part he was more than capable of playing it. There wasn't much that Swayze couldn't do and so it was almost inevitable that sooner or later he would become a big Hollywood star.

He was on Broadway as a young man and then broke into movies. His early roles included Francis Ford Coppola's cult teen drama The Outsiders, the action drama Uncommon Valor with Gene Hackman, and the 'Brat Pack' 1984 John Milius action film Red Dawn. In Red Dawn, the year is 1984. World War III has begun and Soviet and Cuban forces begin an invasion of the United States after strategic nuclear strikes. Elite Red Army parachute divisions begin landing in small American towns and either shooting or rounding up the local population. It looks like Communism has finally won the Cold War.

But wait... not so fast! Help is at hand in the unlikely form of a pre-Dirty Dancing Patrick Swayze, a pre-Hitcher C Thomas Howell, a pre-Platoon Charlie Sheen, a pre-Back To The Future Lea Thompson and a pre-, er, nose-job Jennifer Grey.

The plucky teens head for the mountains and very soon our motley group of brat-packers have all turned into Chuck Norris and are ambushing Soviet conveys and attacking supply dumps. Yes. God bless the eighties! There isn't much of a plot in Red Dawn. The gang become known as 'Wolverines!' and are feared by the dreaded Russkies. Their numbers are depleted by death and one is revealed to be a collaborator. Director John Milius is in full gung-ho mode but just about remembers to tell us that war is overall probably a bad thing and it does have health risks like, you know, being shot for instance. By the end the Wolverines are hungry and exhausted. Rambo meets The Goonies would be as good a way as any of describing Red Dawn. Patrick Swayze is dependable and charismatic as the leader in Red Dawn and clearly destined for bigger things.

Swayze had success on the small screen in 1985 with the miniseries North and South and then in 1987 hit the big time with romantic drama Dirty Dancing. In the film Swayze played Johnny Castle, a dance instructor at an upscale Catskills resort in 1963. His co-star was Jennifer Grey from Red Dawn. Swayze was cast in Dirty Dancing because he could both act AND dance. They didn't want to just cast an actor and then have to have a stand in (as happened in Flashdance - that wasn't actually Jennifer Beals doing the dancing) for the (copious) dance scenes. Swayze was in his element playing a part that required lots of dancing and was perfect casting. The film made him a big sex symbol of the era.

Dirty Dancing was what you would describe as a classic sleeper hit. Not much was expected in terms of box-office but it became one of the biggest grossing films of 1987 and a beloved cult film. Women in particular seem to love Dirty Dancing (which might explain why it sometimes called Star Wars for women - though I'm sure plenty of women enjoy Star Wars too). At 34 years-old, Patrick Swayze was now a bona fide movie star.

Away from the screen, Swayze was happiest riding horses on his ranch and was also a pilot. Swayze was married to the same woman since 1975. He wasn't someone who craved the limelight and had plenty of interests away from acting. It wasn't all plain sailing for Swayze though as he battled alcoholism in the 1990s. Swayze had his biggest ever hit in 1990 with the romantic thriller Ghost. This film, which co-starred Demi Moore, was the biggest grossing film of the year. Swayze was at the apex of his fame. He was supposed to be the lead of Predator 2 too at this time too but had to drop out to recover from an injury sustained on Road House. He was replaced by Danny Glover.

What is interesting about Swayze is the way he seemed aware of typecasting. To this end he mixed up his roles. He would do action films like Next of Kin but then also do family dramas. In fact, after Dirty Dancing he made four action films on the bounce. He later played a drag queen in To Wong Foo, Thanks for Everything! Julie Newmar and even a child abuser in the cult film Donnie Darko. Swayze was famous for throwing himself into his roles. When he made Point Break he insisted on doing the surfing stunts himself.

Swayze's film career lulled somewhat in the years that followed but he remained a beloved cult star. In 2006 he made his West End debut and by now, rather than big Hollywood movies, he was doing things like a King Solomon's Mines miniseries for the Hallmark Channel. Swayze was one of those actors though who was definitely capable of a John Travolta/Pulp Fiction or Burt Reynolds/Boogie Nights style renaissance so who knows what might have happened had he lived to a ripe old age?

At the end of 2007, Swayze celebrated the arrival of the New Year by having some champagne. However, when he sipped the champagne it was like drinking acid and caused him immediate pain. Swayze had suffered from indigestion for some time and it had also not escaped his notice that he was starting to get alarmingly skinny - despite not being on any sort of diet. Swayze had no choice but to do something he'd been putting off. He had to go to his doctor and get a medical check.

The diagnosis was Stage 4 pancreatic cancer - which obviously came as a terrible shock to the actor and his family. Stage 4 means that the cancer has spread to other organs. About 95% of people with pancreatic cancer die from the condition. Swayze's situation was grim because the cancer hadn't been detected early. At the time of his diagnosis, Swayze had just filmed the pilot for a crime drama called The Beast. To the amazement of just about everyone, Swayze shot an entire season of this show despite his cancer diagnosis. It was a testament to how strong and determined he was as a person.

Despite chemo and experimental drug treatments, Swayze was always fighting a losing battle with cancer - although he put up an almighty fight and lived for 22 months after the diagnosis. Swayze slipped into a coma and died on September 14, 2009. He was 57 years-old. The last photographs taken of him were sad to see because this once strong and muscled man was now almost skeletal. Swayze believed his cancer might have had something to do with his chainsmoking and heavy drinking.

Swayze's widow Lisa now campaigns on pancreatic cancer awareness and stresses the importance of early detection. She said her last memories of Patrick Swayze are happy ones of them taking walks on their ranch together. "Grief really sucks, and [it's] very difficult to deal with," she said. "As time goes on, it never goes away. It's kind of like a wound and it heals over, but there's always that scar. And it may not be as visible, but it's always there and you never know when it will raise its head again."

CARL TANZLER

Carl Tanzler was born in Dresden in 1877. He went by a battery of other names though and liked to pretend he was a relative of Countess von Cosel. Tanzler went to Australia as a youngish man but when the First World War broke out he was interned by the authorities there. He eventually went back to Germany where he got married married and had two daughters. Tanzler was quite an eccentric man but he seemed harmless enough. One of his great hobbies was working on inventions. He was always trying to build boats or things of that nature. In 1926, Tanzler moved to the United States. He had some relatives in Zephyrhills, Florida, so ended up here. His wife and daughters later joined him but he eventually left them and took a job as a radiology technician at the U.S. Marine Hospital in Key West.

The details on why Tanzler became estranged from his wife and daughters are vague but it seems safe to say that his state of mind and grasp on reality became increasingly frayed when they were no longer with him. Tanzler was plainly someone who had a difficult relationship with reality. He was plagued with visions of Countess von Cosel from a young age and these visions had shown him a glimpse of a darkly beautiful woman who he believed he was destined to meet and fall in love with. Fate was to intervene at this point and unwittingly feed the delusions of Tanzler in unfortunate fashion.

At the hospital where Tanzler worked, a twenty-two year woman named Maria Elena Milagro de Hoyos was brought for medical tests because of ill health. Elena was darkly attractive and Tanzler was instantly smitten. In fact, he was convinced that Maria Elena Milagro de Hoyos was the woman he had seen in his childhood visions. Panzler believed it was no accident that Elena had ended up in the hospital where he worked. He believed this was destiny and that Elena was supposed to be the love of his life.

It transpired though that Elena had tuberculosis - which was a serious and fatal condition at the time. Tanzler was devastated. He took it upon himself to try and save her life - despite the fact that he wasn't even a doctor. He concocted potions and quack remedies and even used electrodes on Elena in the faint hope that it might cure her. Tanzler showered her with gifts and seemed determined to keep her spirits up.

Elena's family presumably thought it was a bit odd that this radiologic technician was taking such an interest but he was clearly persuasive and trustworthy and they were probably grateful for any medical help at all given the gravity of the situation. As it turned out though, Tanzler's various attempts to cure Elena were purely speculative and had no chance of success. He was simply deluding himself and Elena's family.

His amateurish and eccentric crackpot medical efforts were

predictably all to no avail and she died on October 25, 1931. Tanzler offered to pay for Elena's funeral and her family (who didn't have much money) seemed happy to accept this kind and generous offer. Tanzler arranged for her body to put in a mausoleum but - unknown to Elena's family - Carl Tanzler was the only person with a key to this tomb.

Tanzler visited Elena's tomb each and every day. He brought flowers and even had a telephone installed in the tomb - a move which obviously suggested his mental health was not on the most firm footing. Over the years that followed there was increasing local speculation in the community about Tanzler's eccentric behaviour. It was said that he had become reclusive and was sometimes seen buying women's clothes and perfume. You can probably see where this story is heading can't you? Suffice to say, there was something of Norman Bates in Carl Tanzler.

In the end a rather macabre rumour began to circulate in the area. The rumour was that Tanzler was living with Elena's corpse. Elena's sister Florinda got wind of this rumour and decided there was only one thing to do. She would have to go and visit Tanzler to find out the truth for herself. When she arrived at the house she saw Tanzler dancing with Elena's corpse through the window. Florinda called the police and Tanzler's disturbing secret life was secret no more.

It transpired that Tanzler had stolen Elena's body from the tomb about two years after her death. He had used a trolley to take it home (this was presumably done in the dead of night when there would be few people around). Before that Tanzler would visit the tomb each day and said that Elena's ghost would visit him to sing songs. He claimed that Elena's ghost instructed him to take the body home.

When he took home the corpse he kept Elena in a laboratory and when the skin decomposed he replaced it with wax and plaster of paris. He used coat hangers and wires to maintain the posture of the body and stuffed it with rags. He also put glass eyes in the corpse. Panzler used perfumes and disinfectant to mask the smell. He would sit and have dinner with the corpse each night and talk to it as if it was a living person. He is believed to have slept next to the corpse in his bed although whether he tried to have sex with it is open to question. Some accounts say he did and some say he didn't.

It's probably safe to say that Tanzler was crazy. He said he had plans to build an aircraft on which he would launch Elena into the atmosphere. He believed the heat and radiation would then magically bring her back to life. Surprisingly, Tanzler was deemed fit to stand trial. The charges were obviously for destroying a grave and stealing a body. There wasn't though much anger at Tanzler for his actions. Most people seemed to feel sorry for him. Though his actions were macabre many felt he was just a lonely eccentric. The authorities dropped the charges in the end and seemed to have no appetite for punishing him.

Tanzler was not a murderer or an evil man. He was a deeply troubled man who taken to graverobbing because of a romantic obsession with a woman who was no longer alive. Elena was buried in an unmarked grave (lest Tanzler should track down her body again) and this strange case was put in the past. Tanzler died in 1952. It is said that he built himself a life sized doll of Elena to live with and died in the doll's arms.

THUY TRANG

Thuy Trang was born in Saigon in 1973. Her father was a South Vietnamese army officer who fled the country in 1975 after the fall of Saigon and went to the United States. Thuy's mother was left with Thuy and Thuy's brothers in a detention camp for a time while their father tried to get them over to America. It was a tough start to life and things were about to get even worse. Thuy's mother eventually took her and her brothers to Hong Kong and then to the United States where they settled in California. However, getting to Hong Kong turned out be a nightmarish trip.

They had to stow away on a cargo ship to get to Hong Kong. The ship was packed with refugees and Thuy, only five years-old at the time, nearly died from malnutrition during the trip. At one point she was presumed to be dead and some of the other refugees wanted to throw her overboard. Thuy's mother had to literally force feed her. It was a miracle really that Thuy managed to survive this journey.

They were reunited with their father in the end in the United States and lived in Fountain Valley. Thuy didn't speak a word of English when she arrived in America so had to learn a whole new language. She was a bright energetic kid who enjoyed running and reading romantic novels. Thuy trained in Shaolin kung fu in the United States and got a black belt. Martial arts would be a passion for Thuy throughout her life and her aptitude in this was a factor in winning her big breakthrough role as an actor.

Thuy's father died when she eighteen. She intended to study civil engineering at college and do this as a career but she had a chance meeting with a talent scout which encouraged her to take some acting classes. In 1992 she did a commercial for the Church of Scientology (though she wasn't a scientologist in real life). This was the beginning of Thuy's career in the entertainment industry.

Soon afterwards, Thuy auditioned for a part in the Mighty Morphin Power Rangers television series. The show adapted stock footage from the bonkers kids Japanese TV series Kyōryū Sentai Zyuranger. Mighty Morphin Power Rangers revolves around five teenagers who are given special powers and tasked with defending Earth. They have bright spandex suits in different colours and an assortment of weapons and tricks. The show is sort of like Manga meets the Adam West Batman television show meets comic book superheroes meets Transformers meets Godzilla meets LSD. It was all done on a bargain basement budget with monster suits and miniatures (plus of course some hokey special effects).

Mighty Morphin Power Rangers is one of the cheesiest, daftest, and most surreal kids show ever devised and children lapped it up because it was good tongue-in-cheek fun.

Thuy auditioned with 500 aspiring actors on Power Rangers and was cast as Trini Kwan, the original Yellow Ranger. Audri Dubois played the yellow Ranger in the pilot but they gave her the elbow when she asked for more money - thus paving the way for Thuy to take over.

On the American version they used the stock footage of the Rangers in action from the Japanese show and then had their own actors play the characters out of costume. It was a rather clever way to adapt the Japanese show and make it feel like something made in America. Trivia - Thuy's in costume character from the Japanese stock footage is actually male (which explains why, unlike Pink Ranger, Yellow Ranger doesn't have a skirt).

Thuy appeared in 80 episodes (they really churned this show out at a rapid clip) of Power Rangers and had to move to Los Angeles to make the show. She was by all accounts a cheerful presence on the set and threw herself into stunts that were required. She actually shot a large portion of one season with a sprained ankle but battled through the pain until it was in the can.

Thuy Trang left Mighty Morphin Power Rangers in the middle of the second season, along with fellow cast members Austin St. John and Walter Emanuel Jones. The reason for their departure was money. They were unhappy that they were receiving non-union pay and also not getting a penny of the vast merchandise profits the show was bringing in. The cast felt like they were in something very successful but only getting paid peanuts. Leaving was still a wrench though because Thuy loved Power Rangers and was proud to be associated with something that had so many young fans.

Thuy taught some martial arts classes after Power Rangers and had a small cameo as a manicurist in the Leslie Nielsen spoof film Spy Hard. She had a much bigger role in the film The Crow: City of Angels, a 1996 sequel in which she played a villain named Kali. Sadly though for Thuy, the film bombed and got poor reviews. Thuy planned to appear in some movies with her former Power Rangers colleagues but - frustratingly - none of these projects made it into production.

Sadly, Thuy was not destined to live for much longer. She died on September the 3rd, 2001, near San Francisco after a terrible car accident. She was 27 years old. Thuy Trang and former actress/model Angela Rockwood (for whom Trang was to be a bridesmaid in her then-upcoming marriage to Dustin Nguyen) were passengers in a car travelling on Interstate 5 between San Francisco and Los Angeles. They were returning late at night from visiting Rockwood-Nguyen's maid of honour when the driver (also one of the bridesmaids) lost control.

The car swerved out of control across the road before smashing the roadside rock face and flipping several times before colliding with the safety rail and plunging over the bank. Rockwood-Nguyen (who has claimed both that she was and was not wearing a seat belt in different interviews) survived after being thrown out of the vehicle through a window before its final impact. She suffered catastrophic injuries though and was left a quadriplegic.

It is unknown whether Thuy Trang or the driver were wearing seat belts. The driver survived the accident but sadly Thuy died before they could get her to a hospital. She had suffered dreadful internal injuries in the crash and had little chance of survival. Thuy was laid to rest at Rose Hills Memorial Park in Los Angeles. Power Rangers cast members attended her memorial. In 2023, over 22 years after her death, the special Mighty Morphin Power Rangers: Once & Always was dedicated in her honour, with Trang's character being spiritually passed on in Trini's daughter Minh Kwan, portrayed by Charlie Kersh.

The original Black Ranger, Walter Emanuel Jones, later said of Thuy - "I remember how sweet Thuy was to people. She especially had a way with kids. Her energy drew you in, and her smile made your heart feel safe. I remember Thuy was always getting hurt on set. She put her all into the scenes, so sometimes things happen. I especially remember her having to be carried around a lot due to getting hurt. She was always so positive and gave her all. I'll always remember that about her. She was such a bright light. It's hard to believe she's gone."

KARLA FAYE TUCKER

Karla Faye Tucker was born in Houston in 1959. Tucker was convicted of two murders in Texas in 1984 and executed by lethal injection after fourteen years on death row. She was convicted for killing two people with a pickaxe during a burglary. Tucker had a very unconventional and damaging childhood. Her mother was a rock groupie who got Karla involved in prostitution when she was only thirteen. Karla also began drinking and taking drugs at a preposterously young age. Her father left home when she was very young so she had no role models in her life whatsoever. When Karla was only twenty her mother died of a drugs overdose and left her feeling alone in the world.

In the early eighties, Karla (then still in her early twenties) spent most of her time with a biker gang and on June the 13th, 1983, Karla and a man named Daniel Ryan Garrett went to the Houston apartment of Jerry Lynn Dean. Karla and Garrett were both off their heads on a variety of drugs and much alcohol. The purpose of their visit was to steal Dean's motorcycle. Dean was the former husband of Karla's best friend and Karla seemed to have a dislike for him (it is said that Dean once destroyed some photographs of Karla's mother).

Jerry Lynn Dean was sleeping when they entered the apartment so Garrett hit him with a hammer. Karla Faye Tucker then finished Dean off by striking him with a pickaxe. The duo then noticed that someone else was in the room. This turned out to be a young woman named Deborah Thornton. Karla attacked Deborah with the pickaxe and struck her several times. Deborah was left dead with the pickaxe still lodged in her body.

Karla and Garrett then stole some money and fled. In the space of a few minutes Karla Faye Tucker had brutally slaughtered two people with a pickaxe. She was later recorded on a police wire tap saying that she'd experienced an orgasm each time she'd struck one of the victims with the pickaxe. The police investigation didn't take too long to deduce that Karla and Garrett were the culprits for this gruesome crime and they were brought into custody in a matter of weeks.

Karla Faye Tucker and Daniel Ryan Garrett were both sentenced to death at the trial which followed (Karla had been advised by her legal team to plead not guilty - which was obviously a mistake). Karla said she didn't even remember that night because she had taken so many drugs. Garrett died of liver disease in 1993 before he could be executed.

Karla Faye Tucker, meanwhile, found God while in prison and a campaign to have her death sentence commuted to life attracted support from various people and groups including Pope John Paul II, Newt Gingrich, Bianca Jagger, and the European Parliament. Why all the sympathy for a person who had brutally killed two innocent people with a pickaxe? If you were being really cynical you might suggest it was because Karla was female, white, and quite attractive. These famous campaigners didn't seem to be offering the same sympathy, publicity, and support to black male prisoners on death row for similar violent crimes.

Still, it was hard not to at least have some degree of sympathy for Karla. She didn't seem like a monster at all and while most killers conveniently seem to find God in prison she appeared more sincere than most. Karla wrote a long letter to Texas Governor George W. Bush in which she asked to have her death sentence commuted and expressed her sorrow for what she had done. Karla said she would help rehabilitate other women in prison so that they were better people when they were released.

Bush predictably (and rather heartlessly you might suggest) simply ignored this letter and refused to get involved. He didn't really care if a woman was executed or not. Bush had voters to think about and didn't want to be seen to be being weak on crime. Karla Faye Tucker was therefore executed by lethal injection on February the 3rd, 1998. Karla Faye Tucker had a very basic and simple last meal on death row. She requested a banana, a peach, and a garden salad with ranch dressing. It is said that, despite the frugal nature of her last meal, she didn't even eat much of it.

OSCAR WILDE

'Oscar Wilde,' wrote Richard Ellman. 'We only have to hear the great name to anticipate that what will be quoted as his will surprise and delight us. Among the writers identified with the 1890s, Wilde is the only one who everybody still reads. The various labels that have been applied to the age - Aestheticism, Decadence - ought not to conceal the fact that our first association with it is Wilde. Now, beyond the reach of scandal, his best writings validated by time, he comes before us still, a towering figure, laughing and weeping, with parables and paradoxes, so generous, so amusing.'

Oscar Wilde was born in Dublin and attended Trinity College, arriving at Magdalen College, Oxford in 1874 where he soon stirred things up and began to become famous. Many a dull and dusty dining-table of the era you imagine was suddenly brought to colourful life by a visit from Oscar Wilde. Legend has it that some criminals once tried to rob Wilde in Paris but were so charmed by his conversation they ending up buying him drinks instead!

Wilde is probably most famous for his play The Importance of Being Earnest. The Importance of Being Earnest was first performed in 1895 and remains Oscar Wilde's funniest and most famous play. The play is a satire of Victorian customs and manners and is lavished with many witty and quotable lines and memorable characters. It is split into three acts and begins with the idle Algernon Moncrieff receiving his friend Ernest Worthing in his flat in Half-Moon Street. Ernest has been in the country and wishes to propose to Algernon's cousin Gwendolen but Algernon wants to know why Ernest has 'From little Cecily, with her fondest love to her dear Uncle Jack' on his cigarette case.

Ernest confesses he has a double life. He is really Jack and guardian to young Cecily in the country and takes this responsibility very seriously. But he has invented a younger brother called 'Ernest' who lives in the city and gets into 'the most dreadful scrapes' so that he can escape there and be more carefree when he chooses. Algernon also has a secret. He has invented a fictitious invalid friend named Bunbury in the country who he uses to duck out of tedious social obligations and functions ('Bunbury is perfectly invaluable'). Matters are further complicated when Ernest proposes to Gwendolen, who doesn't know his real name, and Algeron decides to he would like to go and meet Cecily. Someone who will inevitably have something to say about all of these romantic escapades and plans is Gwendolen's formidable and snobbish mother (and Algeron's aunt) Lady

Bracknell.

The pivotal moment in the Oscar Wilde story is course meeting the handsome young Lord Alfred Douglas, the pair soon embarking on a surreptitious love affair despite the fact that Wilde was married with two sons. Douglas introduced Wilde to the world of brothels and 'rough trade' and they were remarkably open about their affair despite the age in which they lived. Homosexuality was regarded to be an aberration at the time, mad and almost Satanic. Never one to do things by halves, Wilde threw himself into the shadow world of Bosie with great abandon although, ultimately, it was the end of him.

'I am a born Antimonian,' said Wilde in De Profundis. Antimonians were a sixteenth century sect of dissenters who believed they were God's chosen people, the elect, predestined for salvation, and consequently they were not bound by conventional moral laws. Apparently, gay people used codes at the time of Wilde to recognise one another, the wearing of a green flower a particular badge of identity. Wilde lent his support to The Order of Chaeronea, a secretive group of intellectual homosexuals who campaigned (furtively of course) to have laws changed.

Wilde believed that happiness lay in immersing oneself in fantasy worlds like the arts, paintings and books. Reality was a dreadful alternative (especially if you had no money). I can see his point really. Given a choice between watching an episode of Stranger Things or waiting for a bus in the rain I'd go for Stranger Things every time. Wilde believed you had to turn your own life into a work of art and seek out pleasure to stave off the mundane boredom of the real world.

Douglas's father, the eccentric and nutty Marquess of Queensberry, eventually confronted Wilde, leaving a card at his club that reads 'To Oscar Wilde posing as a Sodomite'. Wilde sued for libel but lost the case in an infamous trial and served hard time in Reading Gaol, never physically or mentally recovering, his reputation ruined, eventually dying in exile abroad when still only in his forties.

The Ballad of Reading Gaol is a famous poem by Oscar Wilde that runs to about forty pages (in my Complete Works of Oscar Wilde anyway) and was first published in 1898. The poem was written by Wilde when he was in lonely exile on the Continent after being released from jail for 'homosexual offences' and is dedicated to 'C.T.W, sometime trooper of the Royal Horse Guards, obiit HM Prison, Reading, Berkshire, 7 July 1896'.

Charles Thomas Wooldridge, the soldier in question, had been hanged at Reading for the crime of murdering his wife while Wilde was serving time there. It inspired one of Wilde's most famous ever lines for The Ballad of Reading Gaol - 'Yet each man kills the thing he loves'. The poem is very haunting about prison life in this era and contains some of Wilde's most memorable and poignant flourishes. Although not terribly long, The Ballad of Reading Gaol tells a story and also gives you an idea of how awful it must have been for Oscar Wilde to be incarcerated.

Because Wilde was disgraced at the time, The Ballad of Reading Gaol could not be published under his name and went by the author name of 'C.3.3' (cell block C, landing 3, cell 3) instead. The poem received an excellent critical reception and although it was only revealed a few years later that Wilde had written it, from what I can gather in Wilde biographies those in literary circles knew all along who the real author was. It must have been fairly obvious I would imagine to work it out!

Wilde's name was mud at the time and he was desperate for money so getting The Ballad of Reading Gaol published under any name was absolutely vital to him. Few copies were published at first but it became quite popular when it received some very good notices from critics. Wilde himself was apparently never quite convinced by The Ballad of Reading Gaol though, feeling some of the verses were wonderful but that his personal problems and experiences had brought an emotional reality into the poem which he was slightly dubious about.

Wilde also felt the poem went against his theories about art and was generally great in places but perhaps a trifle uneven. Essentially, the poem is Wilde's reaction to the suffering of others and his shock and pity at the terrible things he had seen in prison. His sympathy gives the poem a very poignant and haunting quality, especially the death of the soldier in question. 'They hanged him as a beast is hanged,' says Wilde in the poem. 'They did not even toll, A requiem that might have brought, Rest to his startled soul, But hurriedly they took him out, And hid him in a hole'. The poem conjures up vivid images of a Victorian prison, with lines about warders with jangling keys, inmates shuffling around the yard, squalid conditions and catching fleeting and wistful glimpses of a blue sky. 'In Debtors' Yard the stones are hard, and the dripping wall is high... '

One of the things most interesting about The Ballad of Reading Gaol is definitely the way it gives you an insight into what life must have been like for Wilde in prison. He paints a picture of a fairly grim and somewhat disturbing place where he must have found life incredibly difficult given who he was and how he had previously lived. As you read the poem you imagine a bedraggled Wilde in prison garb as an onlooker to the troubling new world around him and trying to survive and get through each day as best he can.

The poem is full of powerful imagery about iron bars like 'lattice' works, wheels slowly turning and the time ebbing away for the prisoner who provided the main inspiration for Wilde to write this. Wilde writes about sewing sacks, breaking stones and turning the 'dusty' drill. Apart from the line about each man killing the thing he loves the most famous thing about The Ballad of Reading Gaol is that a memorable verse from it was used as the epitaph on Wilde's own grave in Paris. 'And alien tears will fill for him, Pity's long-broken urn, For his mourners will be outcast men, And outcasts always mourn.'

I suppose the only possible drawback to this work is that it is rather bleak and contains not a trace of Wilde's trademark wit and fun. Hardly surprising considering the circumstances in which it was written and what had happened to him in the previous couple of years and this is one piece where Wilde is not attempting to make the reader laugh. The fact that Wilde is writing about the all too real harshness and squalor of a Victorian prison of the era makes the poem more powerful. The Ballad of Reading Gaol is an atmospheric and interesting poem with some legendary verses and is certainly worth reading.

De Profundis ('from the depths') is a long letter written by Wilde in 1897 to his lover Lord Alfred Douglas. Wilde wrote the letter towards the end of his imprisonment in Reading Gaol for 'homosexual offences' but it was only published five years after his death. De Profundis (from what I can gather Wilde called it Epistola: In Carcere et Vinculis but his friend Robbie Ross decided to publish it as De Profundis) is 50,000 words in total and finds Wilde in a reflective and serious mood.

He touches on the arrogance and vanity of Douglas and how he was a bad influence on his work but forgives him nonetheless and also writes about his own downfall, spiritual growth through hardship, and what life is like in prison. 'For us there is only one season, the season of sorrow. The very sun and moon seem taken from us. Outside, the day may be blue and gold, but the light that creeps down through the thickly muffled glass of small iron-barred window beneath which one sits is grey. It is always twilight in one's cell, as it is always twilight in one's heart.'

De Profundis is like a drama as a monologue and is quite paradoxical at times. It seems to lament the fact that he did not break off from his relationship with Douglas and criticises him but is also an attempt to restore relations. Wilde stresses that he was someone who lived for pleasure but those days are now over. 'I did it to the full, as one should do everything that one does. There was no pleasure I did not experience. I threw the pearl of my soul into a cup of wine. I went down the primrose path to the sound of flutes. I lived on honeycomb. But to have continued the same path would have been wrong, because it would have been limiting. I had to pass on.' The letter is always quite poignant because it frequently recalls the past when Wilde was feted by society and wealthy and celebrated and now he is remembering all of this as a ruined man in a drab prison. 'The gods had given me almost everything. I altered the minds of men and the colour of things.'

The most interesting passages in De Profundis often relate to Wilde's own experiences in prison rather than his musings on the role of an artist and how it is noble to suffer. There are some striking moments here, like a scene Wilde paints of having to stand at Clapham Junction, handcuffed and in prison uniform, waiting for a train while people jeered and laughed at him. 'I am really beginning to feel more regret for the people who laughed than for myself. Of course when they saw me I was not on my pedestal, I was in the pillory. But it is only a very unimaginative nature that only cares for people on their pedestals. A pedestal may be a very unreal thing. A pillory is a terrific reality.'

This is a pointed reference to the fact that Douglas had once remarked, while Wilde was ill, 'When you are not on your pedestal you are not interesting.' Wilde never really goes into the specifics of his downfall and writes that many of the things attributed to him by the press and Queensberry were untrue ('revolting malice') but does confess he has also been guilty of 'perverse pleasures' in his life.

Some biographers have said that Wilde's suggestion that the secret of life could be revealed through suffering and there was something noble about sorrow was merely a reaction to his circumstances and dictated by vanity and ego but many of the passages here are nonetheless very striking and interesting. 'There are times when sorrow seems to me to be the only truth. Other things may be illusions of the eye or the appetite, made to blind the one and cloy the other, but out of sorrow have the worlds been built and at the birth of a child or a star there is pain.' De Profundis contains many passages about Christ, who Wilde blends into aestheticism, Christ being someone to Wilde who is a supreme artist and forerunner of the Romantic movement.

De Profundis is a fascinating document and a must read for Oscar Wilde fans. It sheds more light on his life and thoughts about being in prison and finds him in reflective and sombre mood, looking back at his life and knotty relationship with Douglas. It spins off into many esoteric avenues with his usual flourishes before returning to Douglas again near the end. The author is obviously a man of greatly reduced circumstances but somewhat defiant.

There are some moving passages too scattered through the letter like a moment where Wilde recalls someone removing his hat to him as a mark of respect when he entered the courtroom that led to his fall from grace. Wilde is moved almost beyond words by this small act of kindness and says that men have gone to heaven for far smaller gestures. De Profundis is rather short but still has an epic and compelling quality. Anyone interested in Oscar Wilde should definitely read it if they haven't already done so.

Wilde spent his final years aimlessly wandering around the Continent where he cadged meals in cafes and yearned for company, consumed by loneliness. His rapid decline in health, not helped by the harsh conditions of prison, was, according to biographer Richard Ellman, chiefly down to syphilis - although this claim is disputed by others. It was certainly a sad end for someone who gave some much joy through his personality and work.